Principles in Practice

The Principles in Practice imprint offers teachers concrete illustrations of effective classroom practices based in NCTE research briefs and policy statements. Each book discusses the research on a specific topic, links the research to an NCTE brief or policy statement, and then demonstrates how those principles come alive in practice: by showcasing actual classroom practices that demonstrate the policies in action; by talking about research in practical, teacher-friendly language; and by offering teachers possibilities for rethinking their own practices in light of the ideas presented in the books. Books within the imprint are grouped in strands, each strand focused on a significant topic of interest.

Adolescent Literacy Strand

Adolescent Literacy at Risk? The Impact of Standards (2009) Rebecca Bowers Sipe

Adolescents and Digital Literacies: Learning Alongside Our Students (2010) Sara Kajder

Adolescent Literacy and the Teaching of Reading: Lessons for Teachers of Literature (2010) Deborah Appleman

Writing in Today's Classrooms Strand

Writing in the Dialogical Classroom: Students and Teachers Responding to the Texts of Their Lives (2011) Bob Fecho

Becoming Writers in the Elementary Classroom: Visions and Decisions (2011) Katie Van Sluys

Writing Instruction in the Culturally Relevant Classroom (2011) Maisha T. Winn and Latrise P. Johnson

Literacy Assessment Strand

Our Better Judgment: Teacher Leadership for Writing Assessment (2012) Chris W. Gallagher and Eric D. Turley

Beyond Standardized Truth: Improving Teaching and Learning through Inquiry-Based Reading Assessment (2012) Scott Filkins

Reading Assessment: Artful Teachers, Successful Students (2013) Diane Stephens, editor

Literacies of the Disciplines Strand

Entering the Conversations: Practicing Literacy in the Disciplines (2014) Patricia Lambert Stock, Trace Schillinger, and Andrew Stock

NCTE Editorial Board

Jamal Cooks
Mary Ellen Dakin
Korina Jocson
Ken Lindblom
Heidi Mills
John Pruitt
Kristen Hawley Turner
Vivian Vasquez
Scott Warnock
Kurt Austin, Chair, ex officio
Kent Williamson, ex officio

Entering the Conversations

Practicing Literacy in the Disciplines

Patricia Lambert Stock
Michigan State University

Trace Schillinger
Poughkeepsie Day School, Poughkeepsie, New York

Andrew Stock
Vail Farm Elementary School, LaGrangeville, New York

National Council of Teachers of English
1111 W. Kenyon Road, Urbana, Illinois 61801-1096

Staff Editor: Bonny Graham

Series Editor: Cathy Fleischer

Interior Design: Victoria Pohlmann

Cover Design: Pat Mayer

Cover Image: Andrew Stock

Figure 9 in Chapter 3: Data provided by NatureServe in collaboration with Bruce Patterson, Wes Sechrest, Marcelo Tognelli, Gerardo Ceballos, The Nature Conservancy – Migratory Bird Program, Conservation International – CABS, World Wildlife Fund – US, and Environment Canada – WILDSPACE. Original maps courtesy of IUCN 2009. *IUCN Red List of Threatened Species.* Version 2009. 1. IUCN (International Union for Conservation of Nature), http://www.iucnredlist.org.

NCTE Stock Number: 15633

©2014 by the National Council of Teachers of English.

All rights reserved. No part of this publication may be reproduced or transmitted in any form or by any means, electronic or mechanical, including photocopy, or any information storage and retrieval system, without permission from the copyright holder. Printed in the United States of America.

It is the policy of NCTE in its journals and other publications to provide a forum for the open discussion of ideas concerning the content and the teaching of English and the language arts. Publicity accorded to any particular point of view does not imply endorsement by the Executive Committee, the Board of Directors, or the membership at large, except in announcements of policy, where such endorsement is clearly specified.

Every effort has been made to provide current URLs and email addresses, but because of the rapidly changing nature of the Web, some sites and addresses may no longer be accessible.

Library of Congress Cataloging-in-Publication Data
Stock, Patricia L.
  Entering the conversations : practicing literacy in the disciplines / Patricia Lambert Stock, Michigan State University; Trace Schillinger, Poughkeepsie Day School, Poughkeepsie, New York; Andrew Stock, Vail Farm Elementary School, LaGrangeville, New York.
       pages cm
  Includes bibliographical references and index.
  ISBN 978-0-8141-1563-3 ((pbk.))
  1. Language arts—Correlation with content subjects. 2. Interdisciplinary approach in education. 3. Inquiry-based learning. I. Schillinger, Trace, 1969–. II. Stock, Andrew, 1969– III. Title.
  LB1576.S79883 2014
  372.6—dc23
                                                                        2014007865

This book is for our young ones in school:
David, Henry, Maddie, Rachel, Samantha, and Toby.
We wish you rich learning experiences.

Contents

Acknowledgments ix

Literacies of *Disciplines*: An NCTE Policy Research Brief xi

Introduction xvii

Chapter 1 What We've Learned from Teacher-Led Reform Movements in Literacy Education 1

Chapter 2 Teaching Literacy and Subject Matter All at Once, All Together 11
Patricia Lambert Stock

Chapter 3 Transforming Vision, Re-creating Disciplines 35
Andrew Stock

Chapter 4 Spinning Revolutions and Creating History 58
Trace Schillinger

Chapter 5 Learning for and with Our Students 82

Annotated Bibliography 97

Works Cited 101

Index 105

Authors 109

Acknowledgments

As the three of us—Trace, Andrew, and Patti—began to think together about all the students, teachers, colleagues, friends, and family members to whom we are indebted for their beneficial influence on our ideas and the teaching practices we share in this book, we were reminded of the six degrees of separation theory, which argues that everyone is six, or fewer, individuals removed from everyone else on the planet. Not that everyone is a beneficial influence on everyone else. But many are, even when they or we are unaware of their names. Take, for example, William Kilpatrick, the Progressive Era educator, whom we mention in the introduction to this book. We know that the project method of education that Kilpatrick is generally credited with theorizing and advancing has been traced to seventeenth-century Italy and was practiced in the United States in the mid-1800s in manual, agricultural, and general science education by individuals who influenced Kilpatrick's work although he did not know their names (Knoll). So, in truth, although we know we are indebted to many more people—past and present—than those whom we name here, we are especially indebted to and want to thank the following one-degree of separation folks who have influenced our thinking, the teaching practices we share in this book, and our steadfast commitment to our students' learning.

- Our many colleagues in the National Writing Project with whom we have shared, analyzed, and improved our teaching practices; with respect to the teaching we describe in this book, they include especially Sheridan Blau, Cathy Bristow, Nicole Callahan, Stacey Cler, Charleen Delfino, Tim Dewar, Catharine Ferguson, Thor Gibbins, Min-ah Kang, Bonnie Kaplan, Jonathan Lovell, Joseph McCaleb, Roseanne Morgan, Tom Meyer, Kelly Ronsheimer, Cheryl Smith, and Shana Sterkin.

- The wonderfully thoughtful participants in the 2012 NCTE Annual Convention session in which we first published this work, especially Ruth Vinz, professor of English education, Teachers College, Columbia University, who responded to our panel presentation.

- The reviewers of our book, whose thoughtful and perceptive responses to it made it stronger.

- The remarkable students—who must remain nameless—who have allowed us to share their work with other teachers in the interest of our professional learning and who have been our partners in learning.
- Cathy Fleischer, our editor, teacher, and friend, whose commitment to students and teachers resonates on every page of this book. A gift to us, a gift to the field, she's as good as it gets.
- NCTE Director of Publications Kurt Austin, Senior Editor for Books Bonny Graham, and Administrative Assistant Kim Black, for their careful, thoughtful attention to our manuscript; and Pat Mayer, for the wonderfully colorful, inviting cover design of the book.

Up close and personal: From Trace: thank you, Mom, Warren, Samantha, Toby, and Jake, for your love and support, and thank you, my students at PDS, for your energy, willingness to try new things, and humor. From Andrew: thanks to Mom, without whom none of this would have happened; to my wife, Theresa; to my two children, Rachel and Henry, whose love (and frequent day trips to the grandparents) made possible my contributions to this book; and to my students, who continue to teach me what education is all about. From Patti: thanks to the many dedicated teachers with whom it has been my privilege to work; to Heidi, Andrew, and Theresa, now as always: I lucky to you.

Literacies *of* Disciplines
An NCTE Policy Research Brief

The Issue
Consider this: Fourth graders in the US score among the highest in the world on literacy assessments, but by tenth grade the same students score among the lowest. We know that the texts read by tenth graders are longer and more complex, demand greater abilities to synthesize information, and present conceptual challenges. All of these features are compounded by the fact that much of the reading done by tenth graders—actually all students beyond the fourth or fifth grade—is grounded in specific disciplines or content areas.[1]

The discrepancy between adolescent readers in the US and their peers elsewhere in the world and the apparent decline in literacy capacities as students move beyond elementary school suggests a problem that needs attention. A first step in addressing this issue is to examine the meanings carried by literacy and disciplines.

Literacies and Disciplines
Research over the past few decades shows that literacy is not a single or monolithic entity. Rather, it is a set of multi-faceted social practices that are shaped by contexts, participants, and technologies. This plurality is reflected in the many ways terms are taken up and used in research on literacy. For example, a survey of studies published in the *Journal of Literacy Research* found a wide range of meanings associated with the term *context*, which suggests that many related terms, including *literacy*, have multiple meanings. The plurality of literacy extends beyond the print-only world of reading and writing to new and developing technologies, along with visual, audio, gestural, spatial, or multimodal discourses. It is much more accurate, then, to adopt a perspective of plurality, to focus on literacies, recognizing the multiple values and meanings along with the ways literacies are inflected by different contexts.[2]

Disciplines is likewise a complicated term. One complication arises from the fact that disciplines, as they are conceived in higher education, do not exist in secondary schools. Content areas or school subjects in secondary schools are organized differently—social studies, for example, does not exist as a discipline although it is a high school subject—and school subjects often operate to constrain or control how knowledge is presented, while disciplines emphasize the creation of knowledge. Furthermore, while it is possible to identify general qualities—problem solving, empirical inquiry, research from sources, and performance—that distinguish academic areas from one another, the boundaries of disciplines are increasingly flexible and porous. No single discipline can function as a rigidly fixed container of knowledge. As Carter (2007) puts it, it is more productive to "emphasize not disjunction but junction, the intersections of disciplines, the connections between research and teaching, and the ties between writing and knowing. From this perspective, the issue is not so much writing in or outside but writing of the disciplines" (410).[3]

Literacies *of* Disciplines

Developing a New Model
Putting literacies next to disciplines adds another layer of complexity. Traditionally literacies and disciplines have come together as teachers have required students to utilize common strategies of reading and writing in each of their content-area classes. Research shows, however, that this approach does not engender student literacies in multiple disciplines. As Moje (2011) explains, "strategies—absent some level of knowledge, a purpose for engaging in the literate practice and an identification with the domain or the purpose—will not take readers or writers very far" (52). Instead, instruction is most successful when teachers engage their students in thinking, reading, writing, speaking, listening, and interacting in discipline-specific ways, where literacies and content are not seen as opposites but rather as mutually supportive and inextricably linked. When put next to literacies, then, disciplines represent unique languages and structures for thinking and acting; disciplines are spaces where students must encounter, be supported in, and be expected to demonstrate a plurality of literacies. This means taking a much more nuanced approach to disciplines and at the same time affirming the plurality of literacies. As such, all teachers play an equally important role because no one class or teacher can best develop students' literacies apart from discipline-informed resources and lenses.[4]

What Are the Benefits of Literacies of Disciplines?
Research shows that when schools create explicit spaces for students and teachers to discuss the overlap and the differences among disciplinary literacies, teachers become more effective, and students develop new ways of representing and generating knowledge. Learning in the discipline is fostered by multiple literacies, and the learning of literacies is likewise expanded. This process, in turn, enables students to traverse and to transfer learning across disciplines—thus enhancing their ability to become learners who make connections and draw distinctions to function more effectively, whether in classrooms or on-the-job.[5]

Classrooms where literacies of disciplines flourish are nurturing environments for formative assessment. The specificity of discipline-based literacies enables teachers and students to focus on only a few issues at a time, an essential feature for formative assessment because it allows teachers to give students the feedback they need to evaluate their own work without imposing grades. Teachers can use formative assessment to shape instruction based on student progress; considering student performance enables teachers to pinpoint areas where students may need more focused teaching. And teachers in specific disciplines are best prepared to assess student literacies in a given field. The processes associated with formative assessment help students relate new concepts to their prior knowledge in any discipline, making them more likely to transfer learning from one context to another.[6]

What Support Do Literacies of Disciplines Need?
Implementing literacies of disciplines will require significant attention to professional development for teachers. Teacher learning is an integral element not just of the teacher's continuing professional education, but also of student achievement. Teachers may learn in

Literacies *of* Disciplines

varying contexts—through their teaching experiences, school communities, conversations with colleagues, hallway interactions with students, or through professional development opportunities like workshops, inservices, or classes.

Regardless of how they learn, that learning will have a direct effect on what their students are able to accomplish. As the Common Core State Standards (CCSS) are implemented in most states across the nation, new forms of professional development will be required. The CCSS give literacies of disciplines a central position, and teachers will need professional development that addresses how the learning of literacies may be approached within their disciplines.

The professional development that will provide teachers with the resources and strategies necessary to support students in acquiring plural literacies needs to be sustained and systematic because episodic or unfocused learning experiences will not give teachers from multiple disciplines sufficient opportunities for effective learning. One of the most powerful forms of professional development is communities of practice. The National Writing Project exemplifies this approach by bringing together English language arts teachers from multiple schools for an intensive and sustained experience of learning, and research shows that this learning is transformative for teachers and their students. However, for literacies of discipline to flourish, a more cross-disciplinary form of professional development is needed.[7]

How Can We Develop Communities of Practice That Support Literacies of Disciplines?

By working with colleagues from several fields in the context of a long-term intentional community, teachers can become more aware of how their professional knowledge is developed through informal interactions. They can come to see their colleagues as resources for learning, and they can move smoothly between teaching and learning, implementing and reflecting on that implementation with colleagues. They can also gain deeper understandings of disciplinary literacy expectations by reading and discussing publications that address this issue. Experiences like these enable teachers to move beyond thinking of professional development as a one-time event and instead view it as an ongoing, recursive process that improves their own learning across different spaces and contexts. With this kind of professional development, teachers can support students as they learn to explore the multiple literacies of disciplines.[8]

Notes

1. UNESCO Institute for Statistics (2007). *Global education digest: Comparing education statistics across the world.* Montreal. Retrieved from http://www.uis.unesco.org/template/pdf/ged/2007/EN_web2.pdf.

2. Russell, D. (2001). Where do the naturalistic studies point? A research review. In S. H. MacLeod, E. Miraglia, M. Soven, & C. Thaiss (Eds.), *WAC for the new millennium: Strategies for continuing writing-across-the-curriculum programs* (pp. 259–325). Urbana: NCTE.

Literacies *of* Disciplines

Rex, L., Green, J., Dixon, C., & Group, S. B. C. D. (1998). What counts when context counts?: The uncommon "common" language of literacy research. *Journal of Literacy Research, 30* (3), 405–433.

The New London Group (2000). "A pedagogy of multiliteracies: Designing social futures." In Bill Cope and Mary Kalantzis (Eds.), *Multiliteracies: Literacy learning and the design of social futures* (pp. 9–37). New York: Routledge.

3. Carter M. (2007). Ways of knowing, doing and writing in the disciplines. *College Composition and Communication, 58* (3), 385–418.

Heller, R. (2010). In praise of amateurism: A friendly critique of Moje's "call for change" in secondary literacy. *Journal of Adolescent & Adult Literacy, 54* (4), 267–273.

O'Brien, D. G., Steward, R. A., & Moje, E. B. (1995). Why content area literacy is difficult to infuse into the secondary school: Complexities of curriculum, pedagogy, and school culture. *Reading Research Quarterly, 30* (3), 442–463.

4. Draper, R. J., Broomhead, P., Jensen, A. P., Nokes, J. D., & Siebert, D. (Eds.). (2010). *(Re)imagining content-area literacy instruction.* New York: Teachers College Press & National Writing Project.

Langer, J. A. (2011). *Envisioning knowledge: Building literacy in the academic disciplines.* New York: Teachers College Press.

Moje, E. B. (2008). Responsive literacy teaching in secondary school content areas. In M. W. Conley, J. R. Freidhoff, M. B. Sherry, & S. F. Tuckey (Eds.), *Meeting the challenge of adolescent literacy: Research we have, research we need* (pp. 58–87). New York: Guilford Press.

Moje, E. B. (2008). Foregrounding the disciplines in secondary literacy teaching and learning: A call for change. *Journal of Adolescent & Adult Literacy, 52* (2), 96–107.

Moje, E. B. (2011). Developing disciplinary discourses, literacies and identities: What's knowledge got to do with it? In M. G. L. Bonilla and K. Englander (Eds.) *Discourses and identities in contexts of educational change: Contributions from the United States and Mexico* (49–74). New York: Peter Lang.

5. Bergman, L. S., & Zepernick, J. (2007). Disciplinary transfer: Students' perceptions of learning to write. *Writing Program Administration, 31* (1), 124–149.

Childers, P. B. (2007). High school-college collaborations: Making them work. *Across the Disciplines,* 7.

Graff, N. (2010). Teaching rhetorical analysis to promote transfer of learning. *Journal of Adolescent & Adult Literacy, 53* (5), 376–385.

Thaiss, C., & Zawacki, T. M. (2006). *Engaged writers dynamic disciplines: Research on the academic writing life.* Portsmouth: Heinemann.

Young, A. (2006). *Teaching writing across the curriculum.* Upper Saddle River, NJ: Pearson Prentice Hall.

6. Black, P., & Wiliam, D. (2009). Developing the theory of formative assessment. *Educational Assessment, Evaluation and Accountability, 21* (1), 5–31.

Cauley, K., & McMillan, J. (2010). Formative assessment techniques to support student motivation and achievement. *The Clearing House, 83* (1), 1–6.

Pryor, J., & Croussuard, B. (2008). A socio-cultural theorization of formative assessment. *Oxford Review of Education, 34* (1), 1–20.

7. Borko, H. (2004). Professional development and student learning: Mapping the terrain. *Educational Researcher, 33* (8), 3–15.

Whitney, A. (2008). Teacher transformation in the National Writing Project. *Research in the Teaching of English, 43* (2), 44.

8. Grossman, P., Wineburg, S., & Woolworth, S. (2001). Toward a theory of teacher community. *Teacher College Record, 103* (6), 942–1012.

Moje, E. B. (2008). Foregrounding the disciplines in secondary literacy teaching and learning: A call for change. *Journal of Adolescent and Adult Literacy, 52* (2), 92–107.

Webster-Wright, A. (2009). Reframing professional development through understanding authentic professional learning. *Review of Educational Research, 79* (2), 702.

This policy brief was produced by NCTE's James R. Squire Office of Policy Research, directed by Anne Ruggles Gere, with assistance from Elizabeth Homan, Will Hutchinson, Danielle Lillge, Justine Neiderhiser, Sarah Swofford, Crystal VanKooten, all students in the Joint PhD Program in English and Education at the University of Michigan, and Amanda Thompson, a student at the University of Virginia.

For information on this publication, contact Danielle Griffin, NCTE Legislative Associate, at dgriffin@ncte.org (email), 202-380-3132 (phone), or 202-223-0334 (fax). ©2011 by the National Council of Teachers of English, 1111 W. Kenyon Road, Urbana, Illinois 61801-1096. All rights reserved. No part of this publication may be reproduced or transmitted in any form or by any means, electronic or mechanical, including photocopy, or any information storage and retrieval system, without permission from the copyright holder. Additional copies of this publication may be purchased from the National Council of Teachers of English at 1-877-369-6283. A full-text PDF of this document may be downloaded free for personal, non-commercial use through the NCTE website: http://www.ncte.org (requires Adobe Acrobat Reader).

Introduction

The three of us who have come together to write this book—Trace, Andrew, and Patti—imagine you, our readers, to be teachers and teacher educators like ourselves, working in the current moment to do two things: (1) to provide our sizeable classes of diversely prepared students the kinds of content area and literacy instruction that theory and research in our field recommends and (2) to fulfill local- and state-level policy requirements for teaching and learning in our schools. And like you, we're aware that theory and research findings in literacy education, couched as they often are in thick descriptions of teaching and learning, do not always seem to align easily with legislated mandates for literacy teaching and learning, couched as they often are in bulleted lists of learning goals and assessment program checklists. This has led us to ask two questions that we imagine many of you share: What do curricula and instruction look like that are theoretically sound, that are recommended by research in education, *and* that fulfill current legislated requirements for students' literacy and subject matter learning experiences? And, in particular, what do they look like when those requirements named in the Common Core State Standards for English Language Arts & Literacy in History/Social Studies, Science, and Technical Subjects (NGO and CCSSO) emphasize the importance of having students read and write information-rich texts in multiple genres and media? Because these questions get at the heart of the work asked of teachers of the English language arts and literacy today, the National Council of Teachers of English (NCTE) has issued several policy briefs, among them *Literacies* of *Disciplines*, reproduced on pages xi–xv of this book, to support the development of such curricula and instruction.

Teaching Literacy and Subject Matter Together

NCTE's *Literacies* of *Disciplines* brief informs policymakers of a number of things that are well known to those of us who are teachers of literacy. First, literacy is not a monolithic competence. "Rather, it is a set of multi-faceted practices that are shaped by contexts, participants, and technologies" (1; all page numbers cited are from the Web version). Put in the language of schooling: the demands for reading and writing and what counts as effective reading and writing differ in different disciplines and subject areas. In some disciplines, such as the study of imaginative literature, texts in which language use draws attention to itself are appreciated; discourse shaped in extended metaphors, figurative allusion, and onomatopoetic cadences is valued. In other disciplines, such as mathematics, in which economy of expression is appreciated, discourse shaped in equations, charts, and graphic figures is valued. And in still others, such as film studies, in which the grammar, syntax, and organization of moving images are intrinsic elements in the making of meaning, discourse shaped in multimedia is valued. Furthermore, patterns of discourse in different disciplines have traceable historic roots that explain in part what makes them different from one another as surely as do the activities and ideas they inspire and document.

For reasons like these, the *Literacies of Disciplines* policy brief indicates that asking students to use only certain common strategies for reading and writing in their various content area classes does not help students to read and write the different kinds of texts they are expected to comprehend and compose in those different subject areas. Rather, the brief claims that literacy "instruction is most successful when teachers engage their students in thinking, reading, writing, speaking, listening, and interacting in discipline-specific ways, where literacies and content are not seen as opposites but rather as mutually supportive and inextricably linked " (2). For emphasis, and to foreground subject matter instruction for a moment, we want to add another to the brief's claim: subject matter instruction, like literacy instruction, is most successful when teachers engage their students in thinking, reading, writing, speaking, listening, and interacting in discipline-specific ways (see Figure 1).

Figure 1. Ideas from the *Literacies of Disciplines* brief that influence our thinking.

1. The demands for reading and writing and what counts as effective reading and writing differ in different disciplines and subject areas.

2. The patterns of discourse in different disciplines have traceable historic roots that explain in part what makes them different from one another as surely as do the activities and ideas they inspire and document.

3. Subject matter instruction, like literacy instruction, is most successful when teachers engage their students in thinking, reading, writing, speaking, listening, and interacting in discipline-specific ways.

4. In the world beyond school in which we and our students live, few enterprises are defined by disciplinary boundaries; most draw simultaneously on knowledge and practices developed in several disciplines.

The body of educational research underlying these claims emerged in the middle of the twentieth century in the Writing Across the Curriculum (WAC) movement and has since been confirmed and extended in sociocultural and new literacy studies (NLS). In Chapter 1, "What We've Learned from Teacher-Led Reform Movements in Literacy Education," we refer to these bodies of research as we share personal anecdotes that tell the story of how our profession came to understand the reciprocal roles that literacy and subject area learning play in the service of each other. Then, in Chapter 2, "Teaching Literacy and the Subject Matter All at Once, All Together," Patti—a teacher educator—describes a workshop she offers in teacher education courses and professional development settings that draws attention to activities developed and widely circulated in the WAC movement that have enabled us to teach literacy and subject matter, all at once, all together. In the workshop, as participants try their hands at writing-to-learn strategies they might use with their students, they develop a body of knowledge about the subject they happen to be writing to learn about. The subject that Patti asks workshop participants to write to learn about is children's play.

Why children's play? Most obviously, the subject works beautifully in the workshops and in Patti's teacher education classes because play figures strongly in participants' shared experience: everyone in every workshop has some experience and something to say about children's play. But additionally, as participants investigate children's play in talk and writing, the function of role-play in learning inevitably emerges as a topic of discussion—not only as subject matter of children's play that they're discussing, but also as a strategy for teaching and learning about other subject areas. Because role-play figures significantly in how we three teach the literacies of disciplines in our various settings, we conclude Chapter 2—which focuses on the use of literacy practices to produce subject matter learning—by shifting our attention to the subject matter learned. We do this to demonstrate the reciprocal relationship between literacy learning and subject matter learning. A bonus for the three of us who wrote this book is that as we share with you writing-to-learn activities that produce disciplinary knowledge, we also make you aware of a slice of the knowledge that participants produced in this workshop: the role of play in learning. We're hoping this role will be floating around in the back of your mind as we make our argument in Chapters 3 and 4 for role-play as a strategy for teaching the literacies of disciplines.

Boundaries of Disciplines Are Flexible and Porous

Another important fact that the *Literacies* of *Disciplines* brief draws to the attention of policymakers is this one: " [W]hile it is possible to identify general qualities—problem solving, empirical inquiry, research from sources, and performance—that distinguish academic areas from one another, the boundaries of disciplines are increasingly flexible and porous" (1). To this, from our perspective as teachers, we would add: in the world beyond school in which we and our students live, few enterprises are defined by disciplinary boundaries; most draw simultaneously on knowledge and practices developed in several disciplines. Think, for example, of the project to eliminate AIDS that has biologists, chemists, sociologists, historians, geographers, as well as practitioners in human medicine—doctors, nurses, technicians—and social work, and others, working on a common cause. Often this work is described as conducted in the field of AIDS studies. The term *field* in this case is used to signal the fact that in the world beyond school, knowledge is informed by multiple disciplines simultaneously. Likewise, the field of education is informed by psychology, sociology, history, linguistics, subject area studies, and other disciplines. Because we recognize that practitioners of disciplines are also often practitioners of professions, in this book we show how we invite students to role-play by trying on for size the literacies of professional practitioners—such as legislators—born of the literacies of disciplines and moving across multiple disciplines.

As teachers who want our students to participate actively, even enthusiastically, in their learning, we are well aware that schoolwork that captures students' interest and imagination often takes shape in projects that are not only real or realistic but also meaningful to them. More often than not, such projects involve students in interdisciplinary studies, which—from our perspective as teachers of literacy—offer students rich opportunities to discover the value of the subject matter content *and* the literacy practices that different disciplines lend to the project work. It's been our experience that interdisciplinary projects also allow students to discover the differences between the bodies of knowledge and the literacy practices of different disciplines.

To be sure, we are not the first to make these observations. They are rooted in the work of Progressive Era educators such as John Dewey and William Kilpatrick. Kilpatrick gave currency to the term *project method* in his classic article in the field of education entitled "The Project Method" (1918). In the article, Kilpatrick offered a view of teaching and learning intended to serve as an alternative to an efficiency model of education being firmly established in America's public schools in the early years of the twentieth century, a model many critics of current trends in education suggest we are unwisely implementing once again. Instead of lining up as many students as might fit in horizontal and vertical rows in classrooms for lectures, drills, and testing in multiple-choice, pencil-and-paper assessments (the essence of the efficiency model so popular in those years), Kilpatrick argued, we might better prepare students to think, live, and act in a democracy if we conceived of education as part of life, not just fact-filled preparation for it. To do so, he recommended that we engage students actively and socially in purposeful projects in fulfillment of which they would learn to read and write as they *do* history, mathematics, science, etc. In keeping with the values of his time, Kilpatrick offered examples of the kind of project method instruction he imagined: engaging girls in making dresses; boys in getting out a school newspaper; a class in developing and performing a play; students role-playing da Vinci painting the Last Supper or Demosthenes rousing the Greeks against Philip II of Macedon.

While it goes without saying that these are not the kinds of projects in which most of us engage our students today, like Kilpatrick, most of us today conceive of education in school as part of life, not just fact-filled preparation for it. Many of us, ourselves included, design units of study as *projects* to engage our students actively in the discipline-based roles and practices—including literacy practices—that produced the subject matter they are expected to learn. One reason we do this is because, like Kilpatrick, experience has taught us that when our students are interested, invested, and actively engaged in their learning, their chances of being successful learners are dramatically increased. We also do this because, like Kilpatrick, we are persuaded that asking students to assume roles—perhaps not da Vinci or Demosthenes, but instead perhaps wildlife biologists or elected officeholders—enables them to identify with the subject matter we are asking them to learn and with the activities of those who produced it.

In Chapters 3 and 4, Andrew, who teaches fifth grade, and Trace, who teaches eighth grade, offer thick descriptions of projects in which they engage students in twenty-first-century versions of what Kilpatrick called on educators to do a century ago: to play the roles of discipline-based workers and to engage in discipline-based practices as means of learning both the subject matter and the literacies of disciplines. And while Andrew and Trace engage students in inquiry-based projects for these reasons, they do so for other, equally important reasons as well: (1) to learn how the subject matter and the practices—including the literacy practices—that produced the subject matter developed in the first place and (2) to learn how the practices continue to be used to develop still other subject matter. Andrew's and Trace's reasons for asking their students to practice playing the roles of discipline-based workers and to engage in discipline-based literacy practices go beyond Kilpatrick's, however, because they recognize that it is no longer sufficient for students to learn a body of information in school and expect that it will serve their needs as individuals, workers, and citizens throughout their lives. All of us living now—children, parents, grandparents—must be lifelong learners. If we are awake, we know that we live not only in an age of knowledge explosion but also in an age of technological development that enables us to use emerging knowledge in ways that even a philosopher and educator as wise as William Kilpatrick could not have imagined at the beginning of the twentieth century. Citing Nobel Laureate Herbert Simon (1996), a 1999 report of the National Research Council titled *How*

People Learn: Brain, Mind, Experience, and School put it this way: "[I]nformation and knowledge are growing at a far more rapid rate than ever before in the history of humankind. . . . [T]he meaning of 'knowing' has shifted from being able to remember and repeat information to being able to find and use it" (Bransford, Brown, and Cocking 5).

In light of current understanding of what it means to know, we are persuaded that learning the generative practices—including literacy practices—of knowledge making in disciplines is as important to a sound, productive education as learning slices of the subject matter these practices have already developed. Because knowledge is in flux, constantly being updated, students need to learn the practices that make, refine, and revise knowledge. In the chapters that follow, we describe how we make the literacy practices that produce knowledge the subject of critical study in our classrooms and how as students use those practices, often taking on the role of those practitioners, they learn the content required in their subject matter courses.

In Chapter 3, "Transforming Vision, Re-creating Disciplines," Andrew describes a project he developed for a fifth-grade classroom that allows him to integrate all the strands of his required curriculum—English language arts, social studies, science, and mathematics—into what he calls a "coherent narrative." The project, a study of the reintroduction of the wolf into the western United States, asks students to work and think like wildlife biologists, historians, legislators, and policymakers. In the process, Andrew's students raise questions like these: What does daily life look like for a wolf? How do wolves behave? What interactions do they have with other animals? How did wolves become endangered in the United States? Should wolves be protected? Who has the authority to protect them? Should they be reintroduced into the United States? If so, where should those wolves come from? Working to answer such questions, Andrew's students take on the role of practitioners as they talk, listen, read, write, graph, and design texts much like those composed by the disciplinary specialists who actually raised and answered these questions in an interdisciplinary collaboration. In the process, these students also re-create content area knowledge in science, social studies, and mathematics. In other words, by "doing" the work of these specialists in the field, students learn discipline-based literacy practices from the inside out. In this chapter, you'll witness Andrew and his students "pivot" on a foundation of knowledge they construct using the literacy practices of one discipline to understand the literacy practices of other disciplines in order to construct knowledge in them.

In Chapter 4, "Spinning Revolutions and Creating History," Trace describes a quite different unit of study that she developed to engage an eighth-grade humanities class (combined English and social studies) in an investigation of primary documents and discourse practices developed during the American Revolution and other periods of dissent and civil disobedience in America (e.g., the writings of Susan B. Anthony and Frederick Douglass). In a final project, having studied the concepts and practices, including the literacy practices, of revolutionaries, Trace's students investigate and decide on social situations that might move them—or others—to revolution in the current moment. After deciding on a situation they believe calls for revolution, Trace's students develop a variety of purposeful genres of writing—documents designed to announce, describe, and argue for revolution (e.g., pamphlets, YouTube public service announcements, bumper stickers, declarations of independence, constitutions, letters to editors, etc.). They also compose what Bakhtin calls speech genres associated with public discourse (e.g., speeches, debates, etc.). Having studied revolutionaries who made American history as well as the literacy practices they used to do so, Trace's students take on roles and exercise practices that demonstrate what they have learned both about a foundational topic of study in American history and about rhetoric, the bridge that connects Trace's English and social studies curricula.

Like Andrew's students, Trace's begin to learn literacy practices by taking on roles and re-creating genres of writing from the inside out. Rather than being handed a generalized list of "accepted" writing practices, these students compose effective genres of communication in light of the rhetorical constraints facing those whose work in the world shaped the genres in the first place.

In Chapter 5, "Learning for and with Our Students," we reflect together on our preparation as teachers and how we learned to be learners for and with our students in ways that benefit our teaching of subject matter and the literacy practices that produced it. In doing so, we take some time to illustrate how we use formative assessment in our classes to learn for and with our students and how we participate in professional learning communities (PLCs) to learn for and with our colleagues. And finally, we return to the questions with which we began this introduction to our project:

> What do curricula and instruction look like that are theoretically sound, that are recommended by research in education, *and* that fulfill current legislated requirements for students' literacy and subject matter learning experiences? And, in particular, what do they look like when those requirements named in the Common Core State Standards emphasize the importance of having students read and write information-rich texts in multiple genres and media?

And now we begin where teaching the literacies of disciplines began for us, with work developed in the Writing Across the Curriculum movement.

What We've Learned from Teacher-Led Reform Movements in Literacy Education

Chapter One

> *I start with the idea that literacy is not merely the capacity to understand the conceptual content of writings and utterances, but the ability to participate fully in a set of intellectual and social practices. It is not passive but active; not imitative but creative for participation in the speaking and writing of language is participation in the activities it makes possible. Indeed it involves a perpetual remaking of both language and practice.*
> —James Boyd White, "The Invisible Discourse of the Law"

We want to begin this book by describing the Writing Across the Curriculum (WAC) movement that was initiated and led by professional educators in the second half of the twentieth century. Like the current movement to teach the literacies of disciplines, the WAC movement aimed at reforming instruction in schools to benefit students' subject area and literacy learning. Developing as it did at a time when *Newsweek* was declaring to the American public that Johnny can't read or write (Shiels), the WAC movement gained not only widespread attention in our profession but also support from public and private funding agencies (e.g., state departments of education, the National Endowment for the Humanities, the Ford Foundation, the Wallace Foundation, etc.) for professional development in teaching writing in the disciplines and using writing as a means of learning. Perhaps the most notable professional development initiative emerging from the movement is the now forty-year-old National Writing Project.

In a nutshell, WAC, an international movement, called on our profession to make curricular and instructional changes in light of the fact that literacy is a not a singular competence that is learned once and for all, but rather a variety of social practices that are shaped and learned in communities of use across our lifetimes. It also called on us to take advantage of the understanding that language—oral and written—is what James Britton, a leader in the movement, called our most readily available, most powerful means of learning. And it did something else as well. It showed us how to do these things.

Here in the United States, these two calls were addressed in what came to be known as the Writing in the Disciplines (WID) and the Writing to Learn (WTL) strands of the WAC movement. In the WID strand, teachers developed and circulated instructional activities to engage students in the literacy practices that produced the subject matter their students were expected to learn. Take, for example, activities like those Roseanne Morgan, a fifth-grade science teacher, developed to engage her students in empirical observation and description as these processes are conducted in the life sciences. Roseanne invites her students to role-play aspiring adoptive parents of mealworms. After receiving a petri dish of mealworms and information about them, her students undertake a process of observing, describing, naming, and learning how to care for the growth and development of the fragile creatures they will need to convince an adoption agent they are qualified to care for. To document their learning, Roseanne's students compose baby books in which they sketch their charges, noting their habits and development, and write scripts in preparation for role-playing adoption agency interviews. Students in her classes learn the subject matter surrounding mealworms by participating in writing activities that immerse them in the learning, using the kinds of observation and descriptive writing that biologists use on a daily basis.

In the WTL strand of the WAC movement, teachers developed and circulated instructional activities to enable students to learn, among other things, what a recent body of scholarship has aptly named "threshold concepts"—that is, core concepts that, once grasped, transform individuals' understanding of a subject (Meyer and Land). Take, for example, a strategy that Cathy Bristow used to invite students to question their preconceptions about insects in her entomology course. Cathy liked to begin her course by asking students to recall in writing one of their earliest memories of insects. When they shared these recollections, students were surprised to find that their memories proved more often than not to be pleasant ones—catching fireflies on warm summer evenings, gently advising ladybugs to fly away because their houses were on fire and their children in danger. Their recollections prompted students to leave prejudgments, unexamined assumptions, of "bugs" at the classroom door and to enter their study of the insect world with open minds. In other words, writing helped students prepare for content area learning in unexpected ways.

In the chapters that follow this one, as we describe our work in teaching the literacies of disciplines, you'll recognize how deeply grounded that work is in the educator-developed WID and WTL strands of the WAC movement described in this chapter.

Writing Across the Curriculum (WAC)

From 1966 to 1971, a group of educators based at the University of London's Institute of Education—led by James Britton, Tony Burgess, Nancy Martin, Alex McLeod, and Harold Rosen—studied the development of the writing abilities of 11–18-year-old students (Britton et al.). They found that at the time students in most classrooms in England were asked to write for an audience that consisted only of their teachers to demonstrate their learning (usually in essay exams or research papers). Students were not typically given opportunities to write—or, for that matter, to talk—as a means of learning. As the University of London group prepared to publish the findings of their research, they wanted to encourage their professional colleagues to develop teaching practices that would invite students to use talk and writing not just to demonstrate what they had learned, but also to learn in the first place—that is, to explore, discover, complicate, revise, and refine information and ideas about the subjects they were studying.

How they decided to do that is a good story, from our perspective, one that Patti learned when she was having lunch with James Britton some years ago. Britton and his fellow researchers at the University of London decided that their colleagues in the United Kingdom might be encouraged to introduce into the curriculum talk and writing as means of learning if their fellow teachers thought doing so was taking advantage of an innovative movement in the United States. So they named the program of teaching and learning they wished to see take shape in schools *Writing Across the Curriculum* (WAC) because they thought it sounded American and would therefore capture their British colleagues' attention and interest. Turns out, they guessed right. The Writing Across the Curriculum movement caught on in the United Kingdom. Soon thereafter, educators in the United States argued that we had to get on the bandwagon on this side of the pond by introducing the exciting, new British movement into *our* classrooms.

What makes us smile as we recall this anecdote is that Britton and his colleagues didn't coin the term *Writing Across the Curriculum* to promote a program for the teaching of writing. Rather, they wanted it to encourage teachers to ask their students to talk and write for the purpose of learning because, as Britton said in countless settings, language is our most readily available, most powerful means of learning. They wanted to launch what came to be called—on this side of the pond—the Writing to Learn (WTL) strand of the WAC movement.

Writing to Learn (WTL)

In the 1970s, schoolteachers and teacher educators who found Britton and his colleagues' ideas persuasive in light of social constructivist theories of learning (e.g., Vygotsky, *Mind*) began to make them known to one another and to develop a number of instructional practices, commonplace to us today, that invited students to talk and write as means of learning, including small-group discussions in large classrooms, literature circles, prewriting and freewriting activities, journal writing, keeping dialectic (double-entry) notebooks, etc. During the 1970s and 1980s, instructional practices like these were introduced and circulated widely to teachers at all levels of instruction in a host of conference sessions, journal articles, and books (for just a few examples, see Berthoff; Elbow; Fulwiler; Gere; Kirby and Liner; Macrorie; Moffett; Stock, *fforum*). Organizations such as the National Council of Teachers of English (NCTE) and the National Writing Project (NWP) were particularly influential in the widespread circulation of instructional practices that engaged students in talk and writing as means of learning, practices that came to be thought of as the Writing to Learn (WTL) strand of the Writing Across the Curriculum movement: NCTE, in its conferences, journals, and books; NWP, in its institutes, inservice professional development programs, and publications.

An important component of disciplinary literacies, WTL might be thought of as a first step to a fully developed approach to disciplinary thinking. Think, for example, of how Charles Darwin's *On the Origin of Species* begins with the observations and reflections he recorded in his journal during his five-year voyage on the HMS *Beagle*. Those kinds of observations have been re-created in classrooms across the country as a means of introducing students to knowledge in their disciplines. (See Chapter 2 for a description of a workshop that demonstrates the role WTL plays in the development of discipline-based knowledge.)

Writing in the Disciplines (WID)

The Writing Across the Curriculum movement also took fairly strong hold in American postsecondary education. However, its emphasis was different from the WTL emphasis that developed in K–12 education. Beginning in the early 1970s, a number of colleges and universities revised their graduation requirements to include courses that provided instruction in what came to be known as the Writing in the Disciplines (WID) strand of the WAC movement. At the same time, many transformed the most widely required course in postsecondary education, "Freshman Composition," from a course that asked students to write essays about works of imaginative literature into "Introductory Composition," a course that asked students to try their hands at composing genres of writing they would meet in the social and hard sciences as well as the humanities. And while instructors who taught these courses often employed WTL teaching practices (e.g., dialectic notebooks, prewriting correspondences, assigning and responding to drafts of developing papers), their primary goal was to draw explicit attention to the practices, including the literacy practices, of their disciplinary communities as they engaged students in them (see Figure 2). Rather than assuming that students would implicitly make sense of the ways different disciplines construct knowledge by taking courses in chemistry, sociology, psycholinguistics, etc., instructors made as part of the subject matter of their courses explicit instruction in their different disciplines' ways of investigating, reading, writing, thinking, reasoning, and criticizing.

Figure 2. The two strands of the Writing Across the Curriculum movement.

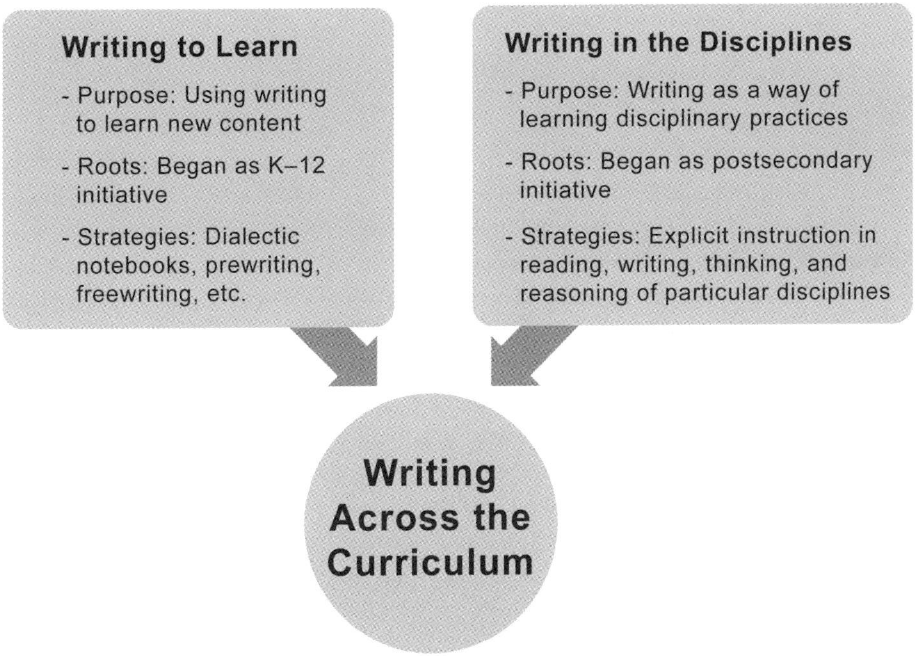

Writing to Learn
- Purpose: Using writing to learn new content
- Roots: Began as K–12 initiative
- Strategies: Dialectic notebooks, prewriting, freewriting, etc.

Writing in the Disciplines
- Purpose: Writing as a way of learning disciplinary practices
- Roots: Began as postsecondary initiative
- Strategies: Explicit instruction in reading, writing, thinking, and reasoning of particular disciplines

Writing Across the Curriculum

We three, and we imagine many of you, were introduced in college settings to discipline-based literacy practices as the WID strand of the WAC movement developed. Patti recalls her introduction to the revolutionary, beneficial impact of the WAC–WID movement on literacy teaching and learning in an article she wrote for the journal *English Education* ("Toward"):

> Winter was giving way to spring when my fellow English teachers and I gathered in a colleague's classroom in Pioneer High School for a professional development workshop. Bernard Van't Hul, the workshop leader [known to all who had the privilege of participating in his workshops as Bernie], captured our attention immediately with an anecdote, an encapsulated tale of one man's humble beginnings, unanticipated good fortune, great expectations; of another man's denied passion; of crime and its consequences. Leaving the end of the story hanging in . . . mid-air, Van't Hul concluded the anecdote with a question worded something like this: "As a result of the events that I have just told you, what kinds of things are going to be written?"
>
> My colleagues and I smiled at the skillful way the professor of English and director of composition had used an anecdote to draw us into a workshop billed as an introduction to developing research and practice in writing instruction and to the University of Michigan's new composition program. As we named the kinds of writing that would necessarily follow the intriguing events Van't Hul reported, he filled the chalkboard in the front of the room with our responses: newspaper articles, legal briefs, letters. . . . When there was no more room on the board, he distributed examples of some of the genres of writing that we had named: an autopsy surgeon's report, a legal brief, a front-page newspaper article, a magazine article. As we read excerpts from these writings and began to discuss the nature and logic of their generic features, my colleagues and I agreed that they were quite different from one another. Van't Hul had positioned us to see for ourselves that although English teachers are customarily charged with responsibility for teaching students to write effectively, English teachers are not necessarily prepared to teach students how to compose some of the genres of writing we were examining that day.
>
> The final piece of writing that Van't Hul shared with us was Robert Browning's dramatic monologue, "Porphyria's Lover," which, as it happens, tells the tale Van't Hul used to introduce the workshop. Acknowledging his indebtedness to Cleanth Brooks, John Thibaut Purser, and Robert Penn Warren for the pieces of writing he used to support the purpose of his workshop, Van't Hul indicated that his argument—and therefore his use of the writing samples—was quite different from the argument that Brooks, Purser, and Warren (1964) wished to advance when they crafted the writing samples and published them in the "General Introduction" (pp. 1–8) to their well-known textbook[,] *An Approach to Literature*. Their purpose was not to illustrate that what counts as effective writing differs in different discourses; their purpose was to make a distinction between *writing* and *literature* (emphasis mine here in print; Van't Hul's, in the workshop). A gifted teacher, Van't Hul used the various pieces of writing, including the one that Brooks, Purser, and Warren identified as *literature*, to argue for the set of theoretical principles he had developed to guide the teaching of writing in the University of Michigan's new writing program.

> Charged with the task of transforming the university's *Freshman English* course (in which students were asked to write about British and American literature) into an *Introductory Composition* course (in which students were to be prepared to write in disciplines and fields across the curriculum), Van't Hul turned the attention of University of Michigan faculty, teaching assistants, and students and of an audience of community college and secondary school teachers across the State of Michigan [and beyond] from models of American and British literature and surface features of writing to classical rhetoric and effectiveness of language use. He made his message memorable with the acronym, MAPS, which he meant to serve as a reminder that all language use (spoken and written) is more or less effective depending on how well it does the following things: fulfills the generic expectations for the **M**edium [speech, writing, visual representation, etc.] or **M**ode (genre) in which it is composed, addresses the needs of the **A**udience and **P**urpose for which it is composed, and satisfies the demands of the **S**ituation in which it is composed. Because his goal was to change teaching practices, Van't Hul chose the workshop format to demonstrate and model both the theory he was advancing and [the] practices he was proposing. According to Van't Hul, his theoretical construct MAPS was "warmed over Aristotle," Aristotle's rhetorical theory rekindled in light of 20th century scholarship in linguistics. (106–8)

Patti remembers that in the enthusiastic discussion following Bernie's workshop, she and her colleagues—high school English teachers all—talked about how much they did not know about the genres of writing they had just examined, never mind how to prepare students to write them. In that conversation, Bernie indicated that similar observations had led University of Michigan faculty to include among its new graduation requirements a junior/senior-level writing course that students would fulfill in their major or a related discipline. He put it something like this: the best place for a chemist to learn to write chemistry is on Chemistry Highway as she breaks beakers, talks, listens, reads, writes—*does*—chemistry with other chemists.

Active Participation in Communities of Practice

In the years since Bernard Van't Hul's observation about the social nature of chemists' literacy learning, scholarship in activity theory (e.g., Vygotsky, *Mind, Thought*), communities of practice (e.g., Lave and Wenger; Wenger), and genre studies (e.g., Miller; Devitt) has argued persuasively and influentially for convictions born of their teaching experience that led postsecondary faculty in the 1970s to take as givens: (1) the literacy practices of disciplines, like the literacy practices of all communities, are social constructions best acquired and learned in those communities of practice; and (2) literacies of disciplines—the patterned, shared ways of investigating, thinking, reasoning, speaking, reading, writing, communicating, and critiquing interactive work—develop differently from one another in the process of serving different disciplines, different purposes, and different goals. In other words, what's considered a sound way to reason in talk and writing in a discipline depends on the purposes and history of the discipline. For example, students learn how to read and write history most effectively when they are immersed in the writing of historians, when they come to see how historians use reading and writing as they themselves read and write in the company of historians.

While this rich scholarship has confirmed, enriched, and extended the understandings of practicing teachers who launched the WID strand of the WAC movement and led to productive changes in the postsecondary teaching and learning of content and literacy practices in the disciplines (e.g., Zawacki and Rogers), it has less successfully secured an influential role in K–12 teaching and learning of subject area content and the discipline- and interdiscipline-based literacies that have produced that content. There are several important reasons why this is so. First and foremost is one described in the *Literacies* of *Disciplines* policy brief:

> Disciplines is . . . a complicated term. One complication arises from the fact that disciplines, as they are conceived in higher education, do not exist in secondary schools. Content areas or school subjects in secondary schools are organized differently—social studies, for example, does not exist as a discipline although it is a high school subject—and school subjects often operate to constrain or control how knowledge is presented, while disciplines emphasize the creation of knowledge. Furthermore, while it is possible to identify general qualities—problem solving, empirical inquiry, research from sources, and performance—that distinguish academic areas from one another, the boundaries of disciplines are increasingly flexible and porous. No single discipline can function as a rigidly fixed container of knowledge. (1)

A second important reason is that usually those students enrolled in colleges and universities, particularly students enrolled in upper-level courses in their major disciplines, have elected those courses. They are immersed in mathematics, for example, because they have chosen that discipline as a field of study. In K–12 education, students are almost always in classes because they are required to take them. They are not necessarily interested or engaged in the subject matter they are asked to study in those classes; they do not necessarily identify themselves as what we might call self-selected players in the game/the field. They may very well not be aspiring chemists, artists, or social scientists—or at least don't yet think of themselves in those roles.

Sociocultural and New Literacy Studies

In her important article "Developing Disciplinary Discourses, Literacies, and Identities: What's Knowledge Got to Do with It?," Elizabeth Birr Moje reminds us of the persuasive body of empirical research conducted in sociocultural and new literacy studies (NLS) that confirms and demonstrates Bernard Van't Hul's and his colleagues' conviction that active participation in a learning community is at the core of individuals' deep learning of the content and practices—including the ways of reading, writing, thinking, reasoning, and criticizing knowledge—of that community (e.g., Gee; Street). Moje also suggests that researchers of literacy learning need to consider the important differences between (1) how and how well young people learn the literacy practices of out-of-school communities, such as fan fiction and video game clubs with which they have chosen to identify (i.e., the young people and the communities that are the focus of most sociocultural and NLS research), and (2) how and how well students learn literacy practices in classroom communities in which their presence and participation is required. As teachers of students in schools and of their teachers, we could not agree more.

Moje concludes her article with a call for descriptions of approaches to K–12 teaching and learning that will lead students to develop the kinds of "deep disciplinary practices, knowledge, and identities" acquired by young people who elect to invest themselves in communities of practice outside of school (70). In this book, we offer three chapter-length descriptions of one such approach. In what we think of as an inquiry-based, project method approach to teaching and learning, we ask students to play the roles of "field-based" specialists in projects that allow them to reconstruct knowledge and recompose the literacy practices of different disciplines. We do this in part because we are persuaded by the wisdom of teachers like Bernard Van't Hul, who said that the best place for a chemist to learn to write chemistry is on Chemistry Highway. And we do this in part because empirical studies published by sociocultural and new literacy scholars have shown us that learners in self-selected, out-of-school communities develop and become skilled in the use of those communities' literacies by using them to solve problems (Gee). Put simply: a century of educator-developed theory and research has taught us that students learn community practices—and that includes disciplinary communities' literacy practices—when they practice them, and they learn the subject matter produced in those communities when they use the communities' practices to produce that subject matter themselves.

Because our students are not learning chemistry on Chemistry Highway but are instead learning chemistry and other required subjects in school, Elizabeth Moje asks an important question that we would put this way: How and when in schools are students' participation, practice, and motivation—although necessary—not sufficient to their learning new subject matter? Is instruction that provides access to already developed knowledge sometimes necessary for students' learning? If so, given what we know about how individuals learn most effectively, how and when do we teachers see to it that our students learn already developed knowledge that their current studies assume? In short, how do we best help students who do not yet self-identify as members of a particular community of practice learn the knowledge of that discipline? Can WTL and WID strategies help in that journey?

As Andrew and Trace describe inquiry-based, project method instruction in which they ask students to play the roles of discipline- and field-based specialists to address real-world problems, they rely heavily on teaching strategies developed in the WTL and WID strands of the WAC movement to introduce students to the already developed knowledge and understandings students need to accomplish the projects. Andrew and Trace describe their instructional approaches and these teaching strategies to invite you to join us in the conversation that Moje initiates, because we suspect that—just as we do—you grapple with how to help students *learn* subject matter they need to know rather than try to "cram" it into their memories for test-taking purposes, only to be soon forgotten.

We begin descriptions of our inquiry-based, project method approach to teaching the subject matter and literacies of disciplines in the next chapter with the description of a workshop that Patti has offered in teacher education courses and professional development settings to draw attention to the role that WTL literacy practices—writing, talking, reading, reasoning, interacting, and criticizing—can play in helping students develop and learn subject matter content. As participants in the workshop engage in these literacy practices to study children's play, they also discover the importance of role-play in learning—the possibility of role-play as a strategy for teaching.

Chapter Two
Teaching Literacy and Subject Matter All at Once, All Together

Patricia Lambert Stock

> *One of the most powerful forms of professional development is communities of practice. The National Writing Project exemplifies this approach by bringing together . . . teachers from multiple schools for an intensive and sustained experience of learning, and research shows that this learning is transformative for teachers and their students.*
> —Literacies *of* Disciplines: An NCTE Policy Research Brief

Several years ago, Sheridan Blau invited me to offer a workshop at the annual reunion of the South Coast Writing Project (SCWriP), which he directed at the time. When I asked Sheridan what issues were on the minds of project teachers, he indicated that teachers in the area were concerned about preparing students to write effectively in different content areas (science, social studies, etc.). As I thought about a workshop I might offer at the reunion, I remembered the one I described in the last chapter, the workshop that Bernard Van't Hul designed to demonstrate that what counts as effective writing differs in the various genres developed in different disciplines, subject areas, and communities of practice. I decided to open the workshop I'd offer at the reunion by reenacting Bernie's workshop as faithfully as possible.

Because those who would attend the reunion were preK–university teachers of all subject areas, I also decided that while we'd begin our work by examining the differences among the literacies of different disciplines, the focus of Van't Hul's workshop, we'd then roll back to concentrate on how such literacies develop in the first place. For even though postsecondary teachers ask their students to talk and write about issues of significance in the specialized vocabulary and language conventions of the disciplines they teach—the importance of which Van't Hul's workshop makes dramatically clear—they don't often take the time to teach their students how those issues actually became significant in their disciplines or how their disciplines' specialized vocabularies and language conventions developed initially. And while it falls to K–12 subject area teachers to introduce their students to the bodies of knowledge produced in the disciplines, they seldom invite students to engage in activities that allow them to discover for themselves why and how those discipline-based learning communities developed that subject matter. K–12 teachers are typically asked to help students master already-developed bodies of knowledge and to demonstrate their mastery on tests, including those that compare students', schools', school districts', states', and countries' educational achievement with one another. This is unfortunate because, as we reported in the last chapter, research in education tells us that students learn best when they are taught how to construct knowledge, not when they are drilled in consuming it.

With this uncovered territory in mind—i.e., how the concepts and understandings underlying work in the disciplines are developed—I grounded the second part of the workshop in activities that would allow participants to discover for themselves how WTL strategies enable learners *to develop and produce knowledge and understandings about a subject even as they prepare themselves to become critical readers and purposeful writers about that subject.* In the workshop, I invited SCWriP participants to try their hands at a number of WTL genres—talking and writing to collect, explore, sort, analyze, synthesize, and communicate information—in a study of children's play, a topic that figures not only in the imaginative literature that is a substantial part of the secondary school English curriculum, but also as a topic of study in many other subject areas and fields as well. And, in a workshop setting where I did not know participants, it was important for me to choose a topic of inquiry about which I could assume that all participants brought prior experience to the table. It was my intention that in the process we would do the following:

- Identify themes, issues, and questions of concern to individuals interested in our topic of inquiry, children's play
- Develop a vocabulary for discussing the themes, issues, and questions we identified
- Develop plans and methods for exploring the themes, issues, and questions that perplexed us about children's play

- Read the writings of others from various fields also interested in and studying children's play
- Examine the various ways in which others have already investigated and are currently investigating themes, issues, and questions of concern to them and sharing their learning with one another
- Begin to write—given our interests and the investigations we choose to pursue—for the purpose of contributing to the discourse about children's play

That is, we would do what specialists in all communities of interest do: we would build a discourse (a body of knowledge) by talking, reading, writing, and otherwise investigating a subject of interest to us. And as we did so, we would not only learn more than we knew about the subject at the outset, but we would also figure out how to continue to learn about it.

Since I designed the workshop for SCWriP's reunion several years ago, I've had the opportunity to offer versions of it at a number of National Writing Project (NWP) sites and in teacher preparation programs across the country. Typically, the workshop I describe here is announced to participants beforehand in a blurb like this one:

> "Learning to Write by Writing to Learn Across the Curriculum" is a two-part workshop. The first part introduces participants to (1) a rhetorical theory of writing instruction, (2) strands of work that led to the development of that theory, and (3) a brief history of the development of major movements (WAC/WTL/WID) in composition studies during the discipline's "explosion years" (1960s–1980s) in America. In the second part, as we use writing to collect, explore, sort, analyze, synthesize, and publish information about a topic of inquiry, we'll reflect on how each is contributing to our understanding of the subject we are studying as well as to the vocabulary, language conventions, and knowledge—the discourse—we are developing to discuss, explore, and shape ideas about the subject.

Learning to Write by Writing to Learn Across the Curriculum: The Workshop

Against the backdrop of Bernard Van't Hul's workshop, which dramatizes the different characteristics of genres in different fields, I open the second part of the workshop by inviting participants to join me in a unit of study titled "Children's Play." We begin by taking about ten minutes to freewrite to the following prompt:

> In as much detail as you can recall, describe one of your favorite places to play as a child. Where were you? Who was there? What were you doing?

As participants write individually, on a piece of poster paper or a whiteboard in view of all I begin to compose a chart that I add to throughout the workshop:

> **Genres of Writing to Learn (WTL)**
>
> •*Writing to* (Re)Collect *Information*

When participants finish writing, I invite us to gather in groups of four or five to share recollections, explaining that our purpose is to add our own to one others' experiences as we gather information about play places and activities. I say something like this:

> Please take turns sharing the memories that your freewriting has helped you (re) collect. If someone in your group reports on a place or experience that reminds you of one of your own that you did not write about, please share that with the group too. Right now we are trying to learn as much as we can about children's play from our collective experience.
>
> Then, when you have finished sharing remembrances, on poster paper we can tape to the walls around the room please chart—in whatever form seems logical to you—any common themes you are finding in your remembrances.

As folks begin this activity, I add to the summary of genres of WTL that I am recording for us.

> **Genres of Writing to Learn (WTL)**
>
> •*Writing to* (Re)Collect *Information*
>
> •*Talking and Writing to Explore and Sort Information*

When time permits, we do a "gallery walk" at this point. Groups visit one another's posters and leave sticky notes confirming insights, commenting on new ideas, raising questions, identifying themes, and so on, and I add to the WTL summary:

> **Genres of Writing to Learn (WTL)**
>
> •*Writing to* (Re)Collect *Information*
>
> •*Talking and Writing to Explore and Analyze Information*
>
> •*Talking, Reading, and Writing to Further Explore and Analyze Information*

In Figure 3 I offer an example of the themes several groups of teachers came up with during a workshop I offered in November 2010 at Teachers College, Columbia University. In professional development workshops, as groups share themes, I note them on poster paper or a whiteboard, asking always, "Why do you make this claim?," explaining that I make this move as well in courses I teach to dramatize for students the need to support claims with evidence in academic talk and writing.

Figure 3. Sample of themes about children's play developed by workshop participants.

> ***Group 1: Places of Play***
> use of surroundings and objects to inspire games of make-believe
> close to home
> "safe" spaces away from adults, but not too far from adults
> secret world
> friends and/or siblings
> weird names for games/places/objects (original)
> invention

> ***Group 2: Common Childhood Themes***
> being outdoors
> physical activity
> absence of parents
> sensory details
> woods
> mess—water, mud
> imagination
> friends
> chasing
> conflict/danger, but security too

> ***Group 3: Themes***
> children determine what is meaningful and valuable
> sense of autonomy
> possibility of object/place
> the setting as a sanctuary (escapism, accessible, self-contained)
> naming of a place/object to establish ownership, exclusivity, privileged
> ritualistic behaviors
> escapism, "magical reality"

> ***Group 4: (No Title)***
> Friends/siblings
> pretend play (use imagination)
> paths to the woods
> outdoors/outside
> risk-taking, not bound by rules

continued on next page

Figure 3. Continued

> ***Group 5: Similarities***
> solitude
> make-believe/role-playing
> transforming spaces
> stayed on family property
> no adult supervision
> indoor vs. outdoor space
> imagination
> siblings

> ***Group 6: Common Themes***
> close to home
> ritual
> no clear purpose
> affordable
> outdoors
> require minimal supervision
> no grown-ups
> imagination
> ownership
> sense of privacy

> ***Group 7: (No Title)***
> transgression
> freedom
> exploring
> gender roles
> siblings
> geography
> make-believe
> dirt
> re-purposing
> destruction

continued on next page

Figure 3. Continued

Group 8: Common Themes
forts
nature
physical
pretending to be grown up
creative/pretend/make-believe
mystique
adventure
safe space
low-stakes risk
sacred or special
stories/narratives
magic and wonder
we "created" the spaces
none of us played with traditional toys
games and rules we organized ourselves

Group 9: Themes
hiding places
outdoors
converting spaces
converting experiences
imitation
create challenges based in place

Group 10: Kids' Play Places
outdoor environments
seasons, weather
group play
imagination
escape
away from parents
acting out stories we read or watched
with family
vivid sensory memories
consistency—every day
setting used to represent various "play stories"—interchangeable
included boys and girls

As we record common themes, we begin to develop a vocabulary for discussing the subject we are studying, children's play. Terms like these emerge:

> Climbing trees, fantasy, playing store, developing identities, breaking rules, pretending, no adults, playing school, playing superheroes, forbidden, make-believe, adults out of sight but nearby, experimenting, making our own rules, dangerous, role-playing, pushing boundaries, trying on adult roles, transforming objects, redefining spaces.

We pause at this point in the workshop as I note that we are developing a vocabulary for working in the field of children's play, just as workers in discipline-based fields develop vocabularies for discussing and exploring topics and issues of interest to them. As we name the conceptual understandings that we are developing together, I invite participants to think about Sigmund Freud's lifetime of work to develop and name the concepts of id, ego, and superego. His was a very different process from the one most students are asked to follow in order to learn the vocabulary of disciplines in schools, where it is all too often assumed that memorizing boldfaced vocabulary words and their one-line definitions in textbooks means that students understand complex concepts (like id, ego, and superego). I ask participants to think about what happens when we reorder customary introductions to new disciplines, when learners are invited to develop and own concepts and understandings rather than memorize names and definitions others have provided them. After learners have formed concepts and understandings, it is easy enough to introduce to them, through writings and discussions, the fact that what they have just dubbed X has come to be known in a discipline or field as Y. By this time, Y by any other name is still the concept that learners developed for themselves. It is now an understanding that they "own."

In both teacher education courses and professional development workshops, as we discuss the array of themes and terms we've generated to account for our collective play experiences, we do a number of other things as well. We identify commonalities across the themes that we named in our small groups, and we discuss similarities and differences in the meanings that groups have attached to these themes:

- Climbing trees, playing store, playing superheroes
- Fantasy, make-believe, pretending, role-playing, trying on adult roles
- Pushing boundaries, forbidden, dangerous, breaking rules, making our own rules
- Developing identities
- Absence of adults, adults not too far away

We also recognize levels of generality in the themes we've identified, and we outline an account of themes in superordinate and subordinate categories like the following:

- **Role-playing**
  - *Fantasy, make-believe, pretending, trying on adult roles*
    - Playing store, playing superheroes, playing teacher
    - Absence of adults, adults not too far away
  - *Pushing boundaries, forbidden, breaking rules, making our own rules*

And while group discussion of the themes we've identified leads inevitably and usefully to layered conceptual understandings and vocabulary development for discussing the subject of children's play, the charts on which I'm recording our work also suggest the forms in which information might later take shape in essay writing. In addition, the collection of charts we've developed always prompts participants to raise questions, such as: *Is play different for children who grow up in rural areas from the play of those who grow up in cities?* And to make claims: *Play is not the same for children today as it was for us. Children today are never allowed to be unchaperoned. Children today play mostly at video games.* As they are voiced, I call claims like these into question by asking: How do we know that? If we can't provide evidence for the claims we make, I reword our claims as questions that I record on the whiteboard or chart paper under the title "Questions for Further Investigation." The following questions are typical of those that develop during our discussions.

- Are there gender differences in play?
- What—if any—influence do geographic settings have on how children play?
- Has children's play changed since the proliferation of computers and computer games?
- Is the kind of play in which "only" children engage different from that in which children with siblings engage?
- Is there a relationship between a child's play and the work he or she takes up as an adult?

As we consider the questions we've raised, we also begin to think together about how we might address them. Discussions like these lead workshop participants to wonder if others have already investigated these questions and to suggest that we might do library and Internet searches to identify books and articles we might read to learn more about the topics that interest us. I always ask in such discussions how *we* might conduct research to answer the questions we've posed. Without fail, as we talk participants identify the shapes of possible studies they might conduct, some of which they discover have, in fact, already been conducted, like Barrie Thorne's highly acclaimed *Gender Play: Girls and Boys in School*. And sometimes, individuals and groups do go on to undertake such studies themselves.

In one case, a group of elementary school teachers in Michigan subsequently asked their students to write about their favorite places to play, who they played with, and what they were doing, coming up with information they then compared to the themes we identified in our workshop.

It is important to note here that while I'm always working at this stage of our study, whether in teacher education courses or professional development workshops, with participant-generated information, descriptions, vocabulary, ideas, and concepts, I also work to *model* the intentional teaching that distinguishes individuals' in-school, instruction-guided learning from out-of-school literacy learning that's been documented by sociocultural and new literacy studies (NLS). For example, when I ask workshop participants to support with examples the claims (themes) I've invited them to name, I intentionally teach a valued convention of academic writing. When I ask participants how we know unsubstantiated claims, I intentionally teach the academy's practice of supporting claims with substantiated evidence. And when I ask participants how we might investigate answers to hypothetical claims, I intentionally draw attention to academic disciplines' reason for being: to conduct research that produces knowledge.

Back to the workshop: with our writing and discussions percolating in our minds, I invite participants to take ten to twelve minutes to write what I call a *correspondence*, a letter to the whole group in response to a prompt I word something like this:

> Please write a correspondence to all of us—if it helps, begin with "Dear Fellow Researchers of Children's Play"—in which you share the sense you are making of children's play. Given what you know at this point in time in our study, what do you think is the meaning or purpose or function of children's play? What is children's play all about?

As my colleagues write, I add another WTL genre to those already charted:

Genres of Writing to Learn (WTL)

- *Writing to (Re)Collect Information*
- *Talking and Writing to Explore and Analyze Information*
- *Talking, Reading, and Writing to Further Explore and Analyze Information*
- ***Writing to Analyze, Synthesize, and Communicate Information***

When participants complete these correspondences, I invite another WTL strategy—"read-arounds":

> In your small group, please pass your correspondences to the right until each of you

has read them all. When you receive a correspondence, please write a brief note, telling the author what you find interesting, what the author has written that had not yet occurred to you, what the author has written that confirms your own understanding, what you'd like to learn more about, etc.

I composed the following correspondence in one of the "Children's Play" workshops, and the responses to it that colleagues in my group offered illustrate the understandings of play that participants begin to develop in light of our writings and discussions, what might be called the beginning of theorizing in a discipline.

> Dear Fellow Researchers,
>
> When children play they re-create the word from the one given them to one they have some chance to shape and inhabit. Students exercise their imagination as they take on and alter roles familiar to them. They become mother, father, teacher, librarian, sports hero, storybook character. They use materials at hand and re-create those materials into items familiar and strange. Sticks become swords; mud and water become potions.
>
> Ironically, although real adults are absent from their play, imagined adults are very much part of their play. Children assume adult roles to experiment with those roles, to test them for fit, to remake them, to discard them, to adopt them.
>
> Play—imaginative play—is more about reality than might, at first, be apparent.—Patti

Response 1: Love [the last] line.

Response 2: Patti, I, too, wrote about how play creates choices and a sense of who we are at that moment. I love the idea of "trying on" roles. I wonder at what age we quit "trying on" and then assume certain roles. How do we know this is the right role for us? It all starts with playing, doesn't it?

Response 3: I loved reading your piece as well as the 1st response. It makes me think about how play is really "serious business." Play contributes or perhaps it is the only means for us to truly understand ourselves and the world around us. I wonder why we don't create new roles? Are there other ways of seeing & being in the world that have not been invented or can we only re-create what we are culturally bound by? Thanks for sharing.

Response 4: I used to watch my son play with his trucks and I'd say he was outside working. Play is work to a child. It's their job and they train & perfect it until they're comfortable. This is what I thought about when I read your piece and reflected on your last line. As adults, we still seek "play." That's why so many adults love to create or be in situations where they can be someone else (Halloween, going out to bars, going into chat rooms.)

Response 5: It's interesting that adults are not present, but their roles are recreated—playing house, school, cops & robbers, etc. I too like your last few lines, they really resonated w/me.

As those of us in the workshop write and share, we recognize how talking and writing to learn positions individuals:

- To be critical, even original, thinkers about a subject
- To have substantial and genuinely interesting information and ideas to share about a subject
- To speak persuasively about a subject because individuals have something to say about it
- To support claims about a subject with evidence
- To be curious and interested to learn more about a subject

In workshops, participants come prepared to write with a variety of technologies (pen and paper, laptop computers, etc). No matter what the technologies in which workshop participants are composing and responding to one another's correspondences, they recognize this practice as a valuable way for students to write and receive immediate, meaningful responses to their writing from several readers. As a side note, practices like this are also low-stakes means for preparing students to write essay exams and final papers. Because most secondary school teachers meet 100–150 or more students in four or five classes a day, WAC proponents in the last quarter of the twentieth century developed WTL strategies such as correspondences and read-arounds to ensure that students would write often and receive timely, dialogic responses to developing drafts of their writing from multiple readers who were genuinely interested in their ideas.

During the read-arounds, I add another item to the list of WTL genres in which we have engaged in the workshop:

> **Genres of Writing to Learn (WTL)**
>
> •*Writing to (Re)Collect Information*
>
> •*Talking and Writing to Explore and Analyze Information*
>
> •*Talking, Reading, and Writing to Further Explore and Analyze Information*
>
> •*Writing to Analyze, Synthesize, and Communicate Information*
>
> •***Writing to Assess and Respond to (Criticize) Information and Ideas***

When correspondences are returned and read by their authors, I draw our attention to the fact that the responses we've composed are first drafts of a genre customarily called criticism, an expression of readers' critical thinking and response to writing about a subject of interest to them. Again, those in the workshop have experienced the genre of criticism from the inside out; rather than being given a definition of the *critical essay*, participants understand the genre through participation in it.

With reference to questions about children's play that we have already raised and those that surface as small groups share correspondences with the whole group, I invite participants—who are now poised to be interested, invested, and critical readers about our topic of inquiry—to proceed in our study as researchers prepared to investigate and contribute to the existing body of knowledge about children's play, a natural extension of the work we've done thus far. Clearly, they are positioned quite differently from learners who might be introduced to the topic of children's play (or any subject matter) by reading and responding to (and often memorizing and being tested on) the work of others.

Having prepared ourselves to undertake a systematic, academic study of children's play by identifying what we already know, what we want to know, and how we might learn what we want to know, we begin our study by (1) reading a sampling of articles published in Elizabeth Goodenough's edited collection *Secret Spaces of Childhood* and (2) imagining a similar collection we might compose based on our experiences, discussions, the reading and research we will do, what we will learn, and what we will be able to contribute to current discourse about children's play.

Emerging from commentaries that participants prepared for a symposium on the topic of children's play held at the University of Michigan in 1998, *Secret Spaces of Childhood* is composed of memoirs growing out of (re)collections like those workshop participants composed to launch our study of children's play. It includes pieces like those workshop participants drafted in the form of correspondences as well as poetry, graphic art, fiction, book reviews, research reports, and persuasive essays. The collection includes articles composed by scholars practicing in a variety of disciplines and fields, such as art, clinical psychology, education, English, entomology, geography, history, journalism, film, landscape architecture, music, philosophy, political science, social work, Spanish, and zoology, as well as by professional authors of fiction and poetry. This variety introduces readers in teacher education courses and workshops to the fact that a field of study, like children's play, emerges from scholarship in numerous disciplines, reminding them of disciplines' porous boundaries. While the authors who contributed to *Secret Spaces of Childhood* often draw on information and concepts developed in their various fields, they composed their articles for a general audience.

When I first discovered Goodenough's collection, I was delighted. I was reminded of the support the WAC movement provided teachers of English in the late twentieth century who argued that it made little sense for our students' essays about imaginative literature, the predominant subject matter of our secondary school English courses, to serve as valid examples of their writing ability when they had few, if any, opportunities to read or study examples of the literary criticism they were asked to compose in high-stakes tests. Read in the context of those concerns, the Common Core State Standards (CCSS) outcomes that ask us to make sure our students have opportunities to read and to compose a variety of textual genres may be seen as taking into account English teachers' professional judgment, not flying in the face of it. A student and lover of imaginative literature and an avid reader of nonfiction texts, I am also someone who has taught young adults, some of whom are devoted readers and writers of poetry and some of whom are avid readers of *Car and Driver* and who try their hands at writing pieces that might be published in it. I recognize this recommendation of the CCSS that was intended to encourage the reading of complete texts, not just textbooks in subjects other than English, as an opportunity for those of us who teach English as a subject to expand the variety of texts and technologies we invite our students to read, write, use, and study critically.

And while Goodenough's collection enables me to encourage the reading of nonfiction texts whenever I conduct this workshop, I actually require it when I engage teacher education students in these activities. In teacher education courses, the collection also serves three other significant functions. First, it invites pre- and inservice teachers to examine critically a genre (i.e., the edited collection) from which they are often asked to teach in their secondary school English classes. Second, with this examination in mind, *Secret Spaces of Childhood* serves as a mentor text, an instructive model for the final text I ask students to compose as a discipline-based research community. And third, it allows me to address Elizabeth Moje's important question that we discussed in Chapter 1: how and when do we teachers see to it that our students learn the already developed knowledge that their current studies assume? While I've invited students in teacher education classes to begin a study of children's play by talking, writing, analyzing, and theorizing their personal and collective experience of play in order to prepare them to study the subject, I wouldn't fulfill my role as teacher if I didn't make it possible for them to learn more and make more sense of our subject of study than they came to class already knowing and able to make sense of. In addition to preparing my students to be successful learners, my job is to foster the knowledge and understandings of the subject we've begun to study that others who have studied it have already developed. Courses of study that begin with "reading the book" implicitly answer the question—how and when do teachers see to it that students learn the already developed knowledge that their current studies assume?—this way: "As soon and as efficiently as possible because there is so much already developed knowledge to learn." But those of us who use WTL strategies to draw students into studies take the time to do so because when students are asked to memorize and define names and terms for concepts and understandings others have developed, those names and terms are often forgotten as quickly as they are "memorized," which means those concepts and understandings are often never developed at all.

In this workshop, to provide participants a sense of how the study in which we've been engaged unfolds in teacher education courses I offer, we read aloud and discuss two brief selections from *Secret Spaces of Childhood*, both of which might have been composed in response to the writing invitation that opened the workshop: (re)collect in as much detail as you are able one of your favorite places to play as a child. In a light-hearted piece, Valerie Miner remembers dressing up in her mother's clothes and role-playing in front of a mirror (Goodenough 51–52); in the other, John Hanson Mitchell recalls how he and a group of his friends trespassed/invaded the estate of a reclusive man in the town where he grew up (Goodenough 52–55). Without fail, workshop participants have already identified the thematic content of these pieces in their own writing and talk. They typically open our discussion of the pieces by comparing and relating their memories and the sense they were making of them to these already-published texts. This is not a point to be taken lightly: workshop participants are reading texts published in the discipline of English studies from the vantage point of developed, shared knowledge. They understand, make sense of, and critique research and writing from the perspective of fellow makers of knowledge in the field. Because they reconstructed the themes, issues, and questions of concern to researchers of children's play in their own talk and writing, they are able to evaluate how effectively Miner and Mitchell address these themes, issues, and questions in the patterns of discourse developed in the discipline of English studies.

Smiling to see the themes and issues we've already discovered in our brief workshop come up in these professional texts, participants and I then turn our attention to how Miner's and Mitchell's pieces are composed, to the authors' craft. Because Miner writes in her voice as a child, as if in the moment, and Mitchell from his perspective as an adult looking back in time, our discussions lead us easily to examine the authors' levels of diction, composing choices of details, images, commentary, etc. We explore how Miner is able to build an adult's understanding of play into a child's lived experience; the philosophic bent of Mitchell's imbedded reflections; and so forth. Time-constrained workshop discussions suggest the complexity of those that develop in semester-long teacher education courses, where we are able to focus on questions of interest in the disciplines of English language, literature, and composition: How do memories become memoir? Why might an author choose to speak in the voice of an autobiographical narrator of limited experience? Of an omniscient narrator? Why compose a piece as a dramatic monologue? Why an essay grounded in personal experience? and so on. In activities at the heart of the ELA curriculum—speaking, listening, reading, writing, visualizing, and designing activities—we take up questions and practices, including literacy practices of the disciplines and interdisciplines that constitute the subject of English: language, literature, and composition.

Many teachers in these workshops have been kind enough to later share with me units of study in which they have adapted these practices to fit their own teaching. One adaptation was designed by Stacey Cler and Kelly Ronsheimer, two teachers who participated in the "Children's Play" workshop during the San Jose Area Writing Project's (SJAWP) invitational summer institute in 2003. Cler and Ronsheimer adapted the workshop into a unit of study, "Let's Play: An Introductory Literature Unit," that they designed to address what were then the State of California's reading and writing requirements for students in their ninth-grade English classes. After beginning the unit of study (just as we began our workshop) by asking students to (re)collect memories of childhood play and to name and thematize them, Cler and Ronsheimer had their students read a collection of fiction and nonfiction articles they had assembled, including several from *Secret Spaces of Childhood*. They engaged their students in reading about children's play in a jigsaw project that they described in the unit of study published by SJAWP:

Literature & Writing I
Secret Spaces of Childhood
Jigsaw Project

1. In your assigned groups, number off so that you each have a number from 1–5.

2. When asked, please find your new group according to your number.

3. Once in your new group, you will be assigned an article. Please complete the following tasks:

    - Silently read the article noting any words or phrases that are confusing. Be prepared to talk with your group to clarify your questions.

    - While reading, also note what this article has to do with the idea of play as we have been discussing it in class. What does this article say about play? Do you agree/disagree?

    - After you have silently finished reading the article, write down at least two questions that you have about play. Your questions can be about any aspect of play that you have been thinking about or [that] has been discussed in the article. Example: Why do we lose our desire to play as we grow older?

    - When everyone in your group is finished, please discuss your questions and thoughts about the article. As a group, you should agree to an answer on the following questions:

        1. What is the article about?

        2. Why is play important?

    - Finally, as a group, compare the questions you have created about play. Pick the three most interesting questions and be prepared to take a summary of the article and these questions back to your original group.

4. Once back in your original group, each group member should discuss the following:
   - Give a short summary of your article. Be sure to discuss overall meaning and how it relates to the larger question of why play is important.
   - While listening to your group members, be sure to add to your notes about play and why it is or is not important.
   - When everyone is finished, share the questions you brought back to your group. Pick what you find to be the three most interesting questions, and come up with an answer to them as a group.
   - Finally, be prepared to discuss with the class your thoughts on play and your questions.

   (Cler and Ronsheimer)

What I particularly appreciate about Cler and Ronsheimer's jigsaw project is that it
- Builds on work they have already done to prepare students to read critically
- Provides students focused purposes for their reading
- Provides students time for sustained silent reading
- Provides students scaffolded small-group opportunities to discuss their reading and refine their understanding of it

While I draw attention to Cler and Ronsheimer's project here because it offers an example of how WTL strategies are used by teachers to benefit their students' literacy learning, in 2004 Cler and Ronsheimer drew attention in their SJAWP publication to how it addressed the State of California's Standards for English 9 and 10 and the State of California's Teaching Standards. All of us today can easily recognize how it addresses the Common Core State Standards' emphasis on providing students opportunities to read purposefully texts composed in a variety of genres and to experience the connections between reading and writing about subject area content.

Although I've had the pleasure of offering the workshop I've described here as a weeklong event, more often than not I'm invited to offer it in three-hour or daylong sessions. As a result, I conclude most workshops by describing how the study proceeds in the teacher education courses I offer in which students read, write, and conduct discussions and special interest studies in preparation for drafting, responding to, revising, editing, and publishing original articles about children's play. These articles composed in a variety of genres become the basis of students' final projects for the course: (1) individually composed articles and (2) individually assembled and introduced collections of all the articles members of the class submit for inclusion in a class book. To fulfill the second part of this project, students read and think critically about their own and their classmates' writing. Each student arranges a collection of her or his own as well as classmates' articles—not unlike Elizabeth Goodenough's collection—and introduces it with a table of contents and an essay that argues for the significance of the collection by claiming a meaning for it as a body of scholarship and by supporting that claim with reference to each of the articles in it. In other words, I position teacher preparation students to try their hands at the kinds of intellectual work in which practitioners in their discipline engage, and in which they might engage their own students as a means of learning and participating in an already-established discourse, a discourse produced in creative and analytic writing and discussion.

The excerpts in Figure 4 from the preface to a collection one student organized illustrate how students typically make sense and compose critical analyses of their research community's writing. Projects like the edited collection I ask students to compose at the conclusion of their study of play position soon-to-be teachers of English as creative and critical participants in the literacy of the discipline they will teach. To fulfill project requirements, after having used reading and writing to learn about the topic they are studying, they write articles in the genres frequently composed in their discipline (poems, short stories, memoirs, analytic essays, etc). They read a body of articles composed in their research community, interpret them, and compose a critical essay that claims and argues for the meaning they have made of the body of scholarship about play—which they have participated in developing.

Figure 4. Excerpts from a student's final collection on child's play.

**Childhood Revisited:
Reflections on the Significance of Play**

PREFACE

I think one would be hard pressed to find an adult who does not harbor fond memories of playing as a child. When we were young, my father loved to set my sister and I howling with laughter with stories of his antics as a boy, and he will still drive two hours out of his way to show us his childhood play places in Chagrin Falls, OH. This loving nostalgia for childhood memories leads one to wonder: What is so significant about children's play? What larger purpose does it serve? In the pieces that follow—poems, essays, short narratives—our contributors seek to answer these questions. This collection of their responses is as multifaceted and complex as the diamond of each of our precious memories of childhood experience.

continued on next page

Figure 4. Continued

Early in the collection we see the work of authors who seek to take us into the mind and world of a child at play. Many of these writers subtly reveal how inherently satisfying play is for children—whether one is a young girl playing "hot box" with the boys next door, or is discovering a family plot hidden in her neighborhood's little wilderness (Henderson's *Not One of the Boys, Not Just Another Girl*, Harlan's *Discovery*). In her poem, "Escapade?Escape," Michelle presents play as "not an act," but "an entirety of focus that mutates reality into something . . . completely free"—one's "own never never land of absent expectation." Indeed, children seem to need that "never never land" of freedom to explore and discover new things—both inside and outside their homes. Amanda's poem, "Saturdays," depicts a child eagerly awaiting Saturday's freedom from school and chores so she can become a "detective, inventor, [or] Racquetball Professional," while Caroline finds freedom to be "the boss" and "a spy" in her favorite childhood hideaway described in *Moss Fort*. However, while Hyatt found freedom and safety—"I was protected"—in her natural fort, other authors reveal the insecurities children experience—fears that adults have often forgotten. With the elegant simplicity and attention to detail characteristic of a child, Susan evokes images of a youth lying awake and alone in the "dark still night," and of a disquieting "musty bare basement/ oozing potato smell" ("Childhood Spaces"). Yet, even among these images is a child "examining, pondering"—exploring and taking note of the nuances of her environment that often go unnoticed by grown-up people. As these pieces suggest, play fulfills an innate need to imagine, to invest the world with meaning, to make the world more full and rich and exciting.

. . . .

The influence of play on choices made later in life is a thread picked up by many of the authors in this second section. AnneMarie's brief memoir, *Faking It*, tells the tale of a brother whose masterful ability to skip school by feigning illness translated into an adult talent for "weasel[ing] his way into upper management with only a high school diploma." On a more positive note, in her essay, Katy thanks her "Cabbage Patch dolls and other stuffed animals for sitting through many days of pretend school as [she] played the role of teacher"—the vocation she would later choose as an adult. Ayasha also highlights a memory of playing school one hot July afternoon in *Nothing Lasts Forever*—knowing that she has now become "the sassy, young teacher" she pretended to be as a child. These memories seem an answer to Scott's invitation to "reflect on one's present position and how it came about" (*Children's Play: A Significant Passageway*). The results of this process—of looking back into the past and realizing the subtle connections that exist between the imaginary world of childhood and the sometimes all-too-real world we exhibit as adults—is what many authors share in their writing. Upon reflection, Scott himself realized that his "ability to see things beyond the literal"—and hence his "love for the

continued on next page

Figure 4. Continued

English subject"—was "due in part to [his] ability to imagine," a skill honed through years of childhood play. Play seems to cultivate an appreciation—if not a need—for aspects of life that are not tangible, rational, or practical. Play opens our minds to the power of imagination in a permanent way. Ultimately, these authors' works suggest play allows children to discover and develop their identity and conceptualize who they want to be in the grown-up world.

As Ayasha's title suggests, like many things in life, children's play is made more meaningful by the fact that it doesn't last forever. The authors in the third and final section of the collection—including Faheem, Alexis, Kristine, and Kayra—rely less on memories of childhood and place more emphasis on objectively explaining the meaning and significance of play. While Faheem's deeply philosophical essay "consider[s] play . . . in service to survival," Kayra's piece defines and sets limits for what constitutes play (*Play as Survival, The Significance of Child's Play*). Kayra makes the important distinction that "when children mistreat others or put others in danger they have . . . left the activity of play and [have] moved into harmful behavior." In *Play or Work?*, Kristine builds on Alexis' *Phases*, and describes how play not only prepares students for later professions—it *is* their work.

. . . .

Play—in all its stages and forms—helps us to develop and mature into the adults we've become. Though there are common threads in all of our experiences of play, our memories are nevertheless unique, and therefore priceless. Throughout life, we carry, and cherish, these memories, and by helping us lend meaning to our surroundings and our lives, play and the invaluable memories it creates render life meaningful.

Why Children's Play as a Topic of Study?

I chose the topic of children's play for the workshop I developed originally for the SCWriP reunion because play is a topic of study in many fields and disciplines, from architecture to zoology, as the essays in Elizabeth Goodenough's collection demonstrate, and because play serves an important, if infrequently discussed, role in learning. And while I designed the workshop primarily to share and invite critical discussion of activities developed in WAC's WTL movement that would allow us to experience how vocabulary, patterns of discussion and inquiry, and methods of investigation are developed in disciplinary communities, I also wanted to prompt discussion of the role of play and role-play in learning.

To do so, after we have talked, written, and begun to read and investigate our way into a study of children's play as that study might be taken up in the discipline of English studies, I often share Jerome Bruner's three-page article, "Play Is Serious Business," published in *Psychology Today* in 1975, to illustrate how play is studied and discussed in the field of experimental psychology. I summarize and quote from the article to illustrate the disciplinary discourse to which the article contributed.

Bruner introduces the article by telling us that experimental psychologists are researchers who study manageable and precisely defined topics—in other words, not topics like play. He explains, "A decade ago, while the methodologically vexed were still rejecting play as an unmanageable laboratory topic, primate ethologists began to raise new questions about the nature and role of play in primate evolution. On closer inspection, play turned out to be less diverse a phenomenon than had been thought, particularly when observed in its natural setting. Nor was it all that antic in its structure, if analyzed properly" (81).

Based on experimental psychologists' study of Jane Goodall's observations of young chimps, Bruner began to wonder whether one of the functions of play might be to make it possible for young primates—including human beings—to practice and refine problem-solving strategies essential for their survival, precisely because play relieves the pressure of a focus on achievement and allows them time and space for experimentation. Informed by the Yerkes–Dodson law developed in his field, Bruner and two colleagues designed an experiment to look at the problem-solving abilities of 3- to 5-year-olds. Children were asked to use sticks and clamps to fish a prize from a box out of reach and were given various kinds of training: some of the children watched an adult demonstrate a technique, some practiced themselves, some watched an experimenter try it, some simply played with the materials, and some had no exposure to the materials at all. Bruner found that

> [t]he play group did as well on the problem as those who saw the complete task demonstrated, and did significantly better than the other three groups. . . . We were quite struck by the tenacity with which the children in the play group stuck to the task. Even when their initial approach was misguided, they ended by solving the problem because they were able to resist frustration and the temptation to give up. They were playing. (82)

After reviewing experimental research studies of children's play conducted in cultures across the world, Bruner concludes his article this way:

> We have come a long way since Piaget's brilliant observation that play helps the child assimilate experience to his personal schema of the world, and more research on play is underway. We now know that play is serious business, indeed the principle business of childhood. It is the vehicle of improvisation and combination, the first carrier of rule systems through which a world of cultural restraint replaces the operation of childish impulse. (83)

In workshop discussions of Bruner's article, we quickly note differences between our workshop approach to a study of children's play through memoir, reflection, and theorizing personal experience and Bruner's experimental study that controlled, so far as possible, all variables but one in a study of children's approach to problem solving. We note how the discourse of writers of fiction and creative nonfiction differs from that of experimental psychologists. We note the vocabulary and topics of discussion and interest that we developed in our short study and those in Bruner's study; and we note the questions and means for further investigation of them that we identified in our study and those that Bruner identifies. With the benefit of time, in teacher education classes, we examine other studies of play conducted and published in a number of disciplines, including architecture, biology, education, history, and philosophy. Just as we do in workshops, in these classes we examine differences among the literacy practices in different disciplines, the interests and questions that inspire them, and the means that workers in these discourses pursue to investigate and circulate their studies for colleagues' review and community use. This approach demonstrates so clearly for practicing teachers and prospective teachers how the literacies of different disciplines differ from one another even across a shared topic of inquiry, an insight that sets the stage for them to introduce these ideas to their own students.

I also share Bruner's experimental psychology article to prompt a discussion of the role of play in learning—and in fact to hearken back to the connection between play and the concepts surrounding project learning discussed in Chapter 1. Without fail in these discussions, we think together about the hypothesis that prompted Bruner's study: play is the business of childhood, children's means of solving problems in circumstances that allow them low-stakes opportunities for trial, error, and success. We also talk about what teaching has taught us: when students have safe havens and opportunities to solve problems rather than being told how to solve them, they combine what they know with their innate curiosity and creativity to learn what they need to know, and, even more important, they remember what they've learned for use at other times in other contexts. Surrounded as we are by charts naming themes we identified in our workshop exploration of children's play, we also discuss the activities we identified as play that we do and can use purposefully as teaching strategies.

I want to focus on one of those activities—*role-playing*—because so many of the excellent teachers I've had the privilege of learning from in NWP summer institutes have demonstrated in their workshops the generative power of role-playing as a teaching strategy for accomplishing what Elizabeth Moje reminds us are the foremost challenges to teachers of subject area literacies: How can we help our students imagine themselves as players in disciplinary communities? And, apart from lectures and assigned readings in which they are often positioned as passive—

too frequently as nodding-off—learners, how can we help them acquire the prior/ subject area knowledge they need to participate in the practices of the disciplines ("Developing")?

In a summer institute of the University of Maryland Writing Project, Catharine Ferguson, a secondary school English teacher, demonstrated a method she developed for students to construct the knowledge they need to participate in a study of imaginative literature. Catharine uses the public television program *Antiques Roadshow* to introduce her students to cultural practices and artifacts in Renaissance England in preparation for their reading *Romeo and Juliet.* She began her summer institute workshop by showing us several carefully chosen clips from the program in which interested owners of "treasured" objects bring artifacts before "experts" to determine whether they are authentic and valuable. In one case, the object is almost priceless; in another, it's a fraudulent copy. My summer institute colleagues and I were as entertained by the clips' unfolding dramas as I suspect Catharine's students are. Then Catharine clustered us in groups of three or four, handed us instructions—as she does her students—that asked us to make artifacts and write scripts that included the expert and one, two, or three people (usually family members) bringing the object to the expert for analysis. To play our assigned roles, write, and play our scripts, we needed to research an apothecary's vial, a letter written in the courtly love tradition, a friar's robe, etc. As we researched, crafted, talked, read, and wrote, we constructed the "knowledge" we needed for a meaningful reading of the play. Our role-plays were often lighthearted.

In our postworkshop discussions, we explored our understanding of role-playing as a teaching strategy by focusing on the pedagogical value of asking students to imagine and compose a "back story" as a means of creating prior knowledge when students' life experiences do not allow them to bring such relevant knowledge to the learning situation. While it is commonplace for good teachers to invoke students' prior knowledge to engage them in learning new material, all teachers are challenged when their students have not had certain experiences and thus do not possess the particular prior knowledge that might prepare them to learn new material. Catharine's workshop drew attention to the value of asking our students to develop back stories as a strategy for helping students who do not otherwise possess it to create prior knowledge that will better enable them to learn new materials and to benefit from new experiences.

Role-playing is a tried-and-true learning strategy for many teachers, one that engages students and immerses them in the subject matter we want them to learn. What I want to suggest, and what we illustrate in the next two chapters, is the power of role-playing to help students enter communities of discourse and to learn the literacies of those communities from the inside out.

With the workshop I describe here and the teacher education course in which it is grounded, my purpose has been to illustrate how the kinds of talk and writing developed in WTL strategies developed in the second half of the twentieth century allow students to discover for themselves the issues and questions that lead discipline-based learning communities to identify topics of particular interest to them, as well as ways of investigating, talking, and writing about their concerns. In the chapters that follow, Andrew and Trace illustrate how role-play in project-based investigations of real-world problems and challenges allows them to engage students in the subject matter and practices of different disciplines and how in the process students discover for themselves the issues and questions that lead disciplined learning communities to find ways of investigating, talking, and writing about their concerns and to develop those communities' discourse.

Chapter Three

Transforming Vision, Re-creating Disciplines

Andrew Stock

> *Fourth graders in the US score among the highest in the world on literacy assessments, but by tenth grade the same students score among the lowest. We know that the texts read by tenth graders are longer and more complex, demand greater abilities to synthesize information, and present conceptual challenges. All of these features are compounded by the fact that much of the reading done by tenth graders—actually all students beyond fourth or fifth grade—is grounded in specific disciplines or content areas.*
> —Literacies of Disciplines: An NCTE Policy Research Brief

As a fifth-grade teacher responsible for instruction in English language arts, social studies, science, and mathematics, I cherish the opportunity I have to devote large blocks of instructional time to interdisciplinary projects. Selfishly, I like the intellectual and creative challenge of searching for ways to "bring it all together," and as a student of history, I tend to assume that reality has already done much of the work for me. My task, as I see it, is to find those current events or moments in history that have *already* drawn my curriculum together. I look for actual conversations that reach across the disciplines, and from these raw materials I develop learning activities that invite my students to become participants in those conversations.

So let's begin with a quick inventory of my curriculum . . . this year. I say *this year* (in an aside that may be familiar to many of you) because I'm a relative newcomer to my school district, and seniority matters. I spent the first four years in my current school at fifth grade; I was then moved to third grade for a year when a section of fifth grade was cut. My next assignment was going to be first grade, but at the eleventh hour I was reassigned back to fifth. So I'll begin with a quick inventory of the fifth-grade curriculum . . . the *current* fifth-grade curriculum (again, in my neck of the woods, and I assume in yours as well, a number of new initiatives are in the works, and next year things will look somewhat different). My curriculum includes ecosystem studies, human impact on the environment, US and Canadian geography, US and Canadian government, and the grade 5 Common Core State Standards for English Language Arts *& Literacy in History/Social Studies, Science, and Technical Subjects* (emphasis added).

As I searched for material that would lend itself to the development of an interdisciplinary project, I was primarily on the lookout for events or issues that had one leg in ecosystem studies and one leg in government. Many things would have fit the bill, but ultimately I zeroed in on legislation relating to endangered species. Here's what I found:

- Gray wolves were once a part of ecosystems throughout most of what is now the United States and Canada.
- By the middle of the twentieth century, humans had almost completely wiped out wolves throughout most of the United States (excluding Alaska).
- In 1973, the US government passed the Endangered Species Act, which called for the conservation and recovery of wildlife populations that were approaching extinction.
- Under the authority of the Endangered Species Act, the US government developed plans to restore wolves to the northern Rocky Mountains of the United States.
- In 1995, with the permission and cooperation of the Canadian government, wolves were captured in Alberta, Canada, transported to the United States, and released into central Idaho and Yellowstone National Park.

History pretty much integrated my curriculum for me; I just had to identify the issue.

Developing this type of raw material into learning activities has many benefits. To begin with, these events *really* happened, and *real* specialists in a variety of disciplines made them happen. The Common Core State Standards (CCSS) call for students to be college- and career-ready. To me it's a no-brainer that teachers should engage students in the kinds of activities that are performed every day by real people who are not only career-*ready*, but career-*successful* to boot.

Second, the actual participants in the wolf reintroduction effort were literate people who engaged in lively discussions about real questions as they searched for real answers. Drawing inspiration from their actual discourse, I find it useful to pose questions like this to my students: "If you're going to bring wolves back to the United States, where are you going to get them from?" This invites students to engage one another in serious discussions. They have to make sense of the situation and understand what's at stake. They have to generate, consider, and evaluate options. They have to take a position, articulate it, and defend it. And ultimately, they have to make decisions that represent their best thinking.

Basing activities on real events also helps me to manage those activities. If students drag their feet on making a decision, I don't give them a deadline and tell them to wrap it up. I say, "There's a team of people ready to go capture wolves—the helicopter is fueled up and ready to fly; they just need to know where *you* want them to go." They get the point.

Another bonus of teaching through actual events is that they leave behind a real paper trail, and that means resources—lots of 'em: books, movies, websites, you name it. All of these are assets to any investigation. In addition, such resources often include examples of the kinds of writing produced by disciplinary specialists. Wherever possible I look for ways to engage my students in that kind of writing so they can participate in the literacies *of* the disciplines as well.

Reality is also a useful tool in the assessment process. Student responses to a situation can be laid alongside the actual responses of disciplinary experts. If student thinking echoes elements of the real discourse (even the elements that didn't prevail), on some level this can, and should, serve as one credible measure of proficiency. I might add that when students become aware that they have "colleagues" in history who have worked on these same issues, they really, *really* want to know how their colleagues responded.

And this is why I design these kinds of units—they allow my students to become participants in a discourse about real issues, utilizing the tools of reading, writing, speaking, and listening to develop an understanding of a situation and craft a reasonable response to it. That's what the work of the disciplines is all about, and—to the extent possible—I want my students to identify with, and act as, specialists in the discipline.

Transforming Identity and Vision through Role-Play

So how do you get a 10-year-old to feel and act like a wildlife biologist? I view it as a process of transformation of identity and vision, and literacy practices serve as both the means of that transformation and a measure of its success.

In his important book *What Video Games Have to Teach Us about Learning and Literacy*, James Paul Gee argues that any deep learning within a discipline requires significant effort and commitment on the part of students. To succeed in their studies, students must first embrace the notion that they *can* learn and work within the discipline, and only then will they make a commitment to it. What does that mean for my Wolf Project? It means that for my students to be successful, they must consider themselves capable of doing wildlife biology, and they must identify themselves, to some extent, as wildlife biologists (Gee; Moje, "Foregrounding").

So how do I make that happen? Road trip. Virtual road trip, that is. No permission slips. Destination—Ellesmere Island, located above the Arctic Circle in the Canadian territory of Nunavut.

To begin the process of transformation, my students and I spend several days pretending to be wildlife biologists on an expedition to study Arctic wolves. Observation is a key component of the scientific method, and we set out to observe wolves in the wild by shadowing a wolf expert, L. David Mech, and a wildlife photographer, Jim Brandenburg, who recorded observations of Arctic wolves in the 1988 National Geographic film *White Wolf*. By crashing this expedition, my students and I get a chance to see a model of scientific practice and record our own observations of wolf behavior.

Before heading north, I show the opening minutes of the film to my class. This introduces them to the climate and terrain of the Canadian Arctic and gives them a chance to size up the filmmakers who will serve as their role models for scientific practice and proper outdoor attire. For fifth graders, much like for actors, wardrobe often plays a useful role in the process of transformation. Sometimes dressing up is so much more than just dressing up. For my students, the very act of donning hats, boots, backpacks, binoculars, and rugged outdoor clothing helps them get into character and "see" themselves as part of the profession. The collective fashion statement creates a psychological point of entry into the practice of the discipline. On the day of our trip, we all come to school dressed for biology. We pitch a tent in the room, spread out sleeping bags, and, with binoculars in hand, turn our gaze to the rugged northern landscape of Canada's Ellesmere Island and the wolves that live there.

Taking on the *appearance* of biologists involves a mere makeover, but identifying with the *work* of biologists involves a deeper kind of transformation. It's the difference between "talking the talk" and "walking the walk." The latter is the literacy of the discipline—the human interactions that are at the very heart of the production of knowledge in science. In the case of this project, those interactions are rooted in the collection, analysis, and presentation of evidence regarding wolf behavior.

One of *White Wolf*'s virtues, from my perspective, is the great model it provides for the literacy practices that scientists use to create knowledge. The biologist in the film, Dave Mech, frequently appears on camera jotting observations into notebooks of all shapes and sizes. Not to be outdone by the Dave Mechs of the world, my students and I create our own field notebooks from construction paper and the abundant supply of yellow-lined paper our school overordered several years ago.

As we staple the pages together, I can't help but think back to the summer of 1994 when I purchased my first Rite in the Rain notebook. I had registered for some ecology courses at the University of Michigan Biological Station, and the notebook was on the list of required supplies. Somehow I'd managed to make it through thirteen years of public school and four years of college without realizing that waterproof paper even existed, but as soon as I began to *do* ecology, I understood why it had been invented. I found myself working under conditions I had never previously encountered as a writer. I wrote in drizzles and steady downpours. I scribbled notes while wading through streams, and I recorded observations while handling insects, snails, and crayfish. As I think about literacy in science, those notebooks remind me that the very instruments of writing, including paper itself, have been adapted over time to meet the specific needs of disciplines. When I purchased my first Rite in the Rain notebook, I knew that I was entering a world in which I would be expected to write *in* nature, without a desk, while soaking wet. For me, that was a new kind of literacy.

When my students finally put their notebooks to use, my instructions on what to record are very general. I ask that everyone be on the lookout for information that might address the following questions: "What is this part of the world like?" and "What are the wolves doing?" We then view the film silently (with no captions). Why silently? A silent viewing more closely approximates the conditions under which the filmmakers made their own observations. Nobody was narrating for them, nor was there a sound track playing in the background to elicit emotional responses to the scenes they witnessed. The silence forces students to be keen observers. They watch the film intently because the visual images are their only source of information. The absence of a running narrative also requires students to make sense of events on their own terms and in their own words, free from the influence of the filmmakers' commentary. A picture is worth a thousand words, and as a teacher I want to know what those thousand words are for each of my students.

I break the viewing of the film into short segments of four to five minutes each, which helps us manage the task of note-taking. Frequent pauses give students time to record their thoughts in writing without missing any of the action. They take notes using a double-entry format: the right-hand pages of their notebooks are for their observations; the left-hand pages are reserved for future notes to be added during a second, "ears on" presentation of the film. Notes for each segment are recorded on a separate page and labeled, for future reference, with a segment number that I provide.

Breaking the film into segments has other advantages as well. After all, the events documented in the film were spread out over time for the original observers. This gave them the opportunity to talk about what they had seen and to shape their understanding of it. To their credit, the filmmakers recorded many of these rich conversations, and the students understand exactly what those conversations are about, even when the sound is off. Not to be outdone by the Mechs and Brandenburgs of the world, we *also* hold conversations at the end of each segment to make sense of what *we* have seen.

After discussing a segment with a partner, students share their observations with the whole group, and I record each new observation on chart paper. For struggling students, this provides an opportunity to hear what others saw in the segment, and it provides guidance for what to look for in the next segment. The groupthink has two other benefits as well. It gives students a chance to "publish" their own ideas, and it gives me an opportunity to demonstrate how to take notes using a bullet-point format—a model that many students immediately begin to pick up on and use.

The first day of observations is intense. The running time of the film is approximately fifty minutes, but with periodic interruptions for partner conversations and whole-group discussions, it takes several hours to complete the film. When we return to school for the second day of activity—this time in our usual attire—we view the same film again, but this time with the sound on.

Before watching each segment as a rerun, I ask students to read through their notes from the previous day, a task made easier by the fact that we labeled each page in the notebook with the appropriate segment number. The purpose of watching the reruns is to draw additional voices into the discussion of wolves—the voices of specialists who approach the subject with the vocabulary and conceptual understanding of wildlife biologists. Discovering similarities between their observations and those of the professionals bolsters students' emerging sense of themselves as biologists. When they encounter differences in perspective and vocabulary, the differences serve as occasions to reflect on, reconsider, and (in some cases) revise their original notes.

Frankly, I delight in the revisions. They are the most visible trail I have of the evolution of each student's thinking. To make this trail easier to follow, I instruct students to make their notebook entries in pencil on the first day and in pen on the second day. One student made the following entry on the first day: "two wolves with their babies in a cave." By the end of the second day, that entry had been revised to read: "two wolves with their ~~babies~~ **pups** in a ~~cave~~ **den**." In the case of another student, the entries for day 2 contained a variety of words that were altogether absent from the notebook on day 1. This new vocabulary included such words as *musk oxen* (which replaced *yaks* in the original), *calf* (which replaced *little yak*), *litter, nursing, regurgitation, alpha male, alpha female, ranking*, and *territorial*. This acquisition of domain-specific vocabulary—Tier 3 words, as the CCSS refer to them—is one way the reruns support and enhance students' ability to participate in a discourse about wolves.

The process of transformation, however, is not limited to mere word-for-word substitutions. On day 2, students not only describe things differently but they also *see* things differently. During the first viewing of the film, one student recorded the brief observation: "wolf peeing." For most 10-year-olds, the scene that inspired this entry is appreciated largely in terms of its comedic (rather than scientific) value. However, when the students are able to hear the filmmaker's take on the situation, they learn that urinating with a raised leg is one way an alpha (or dominant) wolf demonstrates its leadership within the pack. Accordingly, the author of "wolf peeing" made revisions on day 2 to incorporate details of the wolf's social status, as well as the key gesture that the filmmakers cited as evidence of its position within the pack: "~~wolf~~ **alpha male** peeing **w/ one leg up**."

In a sense, this is what an education in a discipline is all about—a "transformation of vision" in which students develop a view of nature that is shared by real practitioners of the discipline. As Thomas Kuhn argues in his influential book *The Structure of Scientific Revolutions*: "[N]ature is too complex and varied to be explored at random" (109). Disciplines arise in response to this challenge, and people develop ideas about which aspects of nature are worth studying—ideas that guide them in their observations and experiments. Identifying with a discipline in this sense involves learning to *see* the world through the lens of the discipline, focusing narrowly on the particular entities, phenomena, concepts, and questions that the discipline considers relevant to the study of nature. The student who observes a wolf relieving itself on day 1 but sees evidence of social hierarchy by the end of day 2 has begun to see the world of wolves differently. As Kuhn notes: "Only after a number of such transformations of vision does the student become an inhabitant of the scientist's world, seeing what the scientist sees and responding as the scientist does" (111). This is why I do transformations of vision for a living.

Turning Observations into Text

At the conclusion of day 2, students have in their possession notebooks loaded with new information and vocabulary, organized chronologically by film segment. During the next phase of the project, they begin to organize these observations in terms of content—grouping related facts and identifying categories of information.

This process begins with an "observation slap." In a nutshell, students work with partners to record an observation from their notes and then slap it up on a magnetic whiteboard for the whole class to see. This work involves some discussion and decision making, and with the whole class working on the project, we cover territory pretty quickly. I give the students a moment to review everyone's work and consolidate any duplicated items. Then a second round of postings begins with the following condition: "You can't post anything that's already been posted. New stuff only." The slapping continues through multiple rounds until the observations have been largely exhausted. Be advised: there will be clutter.

Once all the observations are in, it's time to sort them into categories. "Do you see any observations that seem like they belong together in a group?" I ask. Partners survey the board in search of related observations. They pull two related observations to start a new group or move one observation over to an existing group. The sorting continues until every observation has a new home in a group. I view this process as one of sifting and separating—which is both a metaphor for critical thinking as well as the origin of the term itself. The word *critical* evolved from ancient words for "sieve" and the related actions of separating, deciding, and judging. When I ask my students to sift through a pile of observations and group ideas with related content, I'm basically asking them to develop criteria (another sieve-related term) for membership in the group. This requires some reading, some thinking, and a fair amount of discussion—a perfect prelude to writing.

So what did my class come up with for categories? By the time the dust had settled, the observations all fell under one of the following headings: where wolves live, social organization, pups, prey, territorial behavior, and wolves and humans. Building on their work, I asked the students to write a description of the wolves of Ellesmere Island that would include a section for each of the categories they had developed. I left the categories up on the whiteboard for all to see, but I removed the observations. This forced the students to produce a text from what they now knew—copying was simply not an option.

Was this a summative assessment? Sure. I wanted to see what they had learned from observing wolves. But that's not the whole story. I had not yet done any direct instruction on producing a text with sections devoted to various categories of information. In that respect, the assessment was formative and would guide future instruction in writing.

So I gave the assignment and waited for the results to come in. When we paused for a midmorning snack, I recorded some observations in a voice memo on my iPhone:

> I'm really impressed with the amount of writing that was happening here with the Wolf Project. People were busy, I want to say, for like . . . a half an hour of sustained

> writing. There were a lot of people really writing. That whole *writing floats on a sea of talk* thing, I think this was a perfect illustration of that. Without all of that talk that came before it, there's no way they would have been able to produce this stuff. They were very good at maintaining a high level of involvement in this. There were the exceptions, of course. But [overall] that was great. It was very good to see.

This moment remains the clearest example from my own teaching of James Britton's powerful notion that "[t]alk is the sea upon which all else floats" (164). Talk was an important part of our initial observation activities and a key element in the posting of facts, as well as in the subsequent sorting of those facts into categories. It was at the heart of everything we had done, and when the students finally sat down to write, those conversations were with them. I don't think it's an exaggeration to say that I'll never look at talk the same way again. Britton's words, and the talkers in my classroom, have changed the way I view literacy and instruction.

This marked the conclusion of our journey to Ellesmere Island. We came, we saw, we produced knowledge in the discipline. As I reflected on the journey, I knew that I had tangible evidence of the success of our expedition in the written work of my students. Nonetheless, I couldn't help but wonder if they *felt* like biologists. Unable to think of a better way to measure this, I put the question to them directly. Some said, "Yes," others pointed out that we hadn't done any *real* biology. After all, watching animals on a TV screen just isn't the same as observing them in real life.

It was a fair statement. What was my response? Backyard biology. I asked my students to work individually or with a partner to make observations of wildlife in their yard or at some other safe location. Much like Dave Mech, they had to maintain a field notebook with their observations, and much like Jim Brandenburg, they had to gather evidence of the presence of wildlife in their location in the form of photographs or drawings. Since the observations had to be made at home, I wrote a letter to parents outlining the purpose and expectations of the assignment (see Figure 5).

Unlike our Ellesmere observations, real observation requires time and patience. While conducting a preliminary review of some of the field notebooks, I realized that when patience was in short supply, Web searches were being used to fill the void. For instance, several students had information on the average weight of a deer.

"Did you actually weigh a deer?" I asked.

"No," was the universal response.

"For this project, we are going to limit the information to the things you can back up with your own observations."

Bit by bit, students (and parents) began to see that this assignment was not a "species report," in which the observations of others would play a role. The

Figure 5. Letter to parents explaining the Backyard Biology assignment.

Backyard Biology Project

Background

During the first half of the year, we have been working as biologists-in-training. As we progressed through our studies, I posed the question to students: "Do you *feel* like a biologist?" The responses showed that although students felt they had some foundation in the study of biology, they hadn't yet gone out into nature to make direct observations of wildlife. This project, which came from student suggestions, seeks to address that issue.

The Assignment: Backyard Biology

Students may work individually, or with a partner from the class, to make observations of wildlife in their yard, or in some other nearby area that they can safely access on a regular basis. If the work is to be done with a partner, the observations can be made at two different locations—the yards of both students, for example. Observations can be made from indoors looking out, or by exploring outside. The second floor windows in my house give me a great view of my backyard! Safety and warmth are important considerations at this time of year.

- Students must maintain and hand in a field notebook in which they document their observations.

    o What animals do you see?
     - What do they look like?
     - Where do you see them?
     - What are they doing?

    o What signs of animal life do you see?
     - Tracks
     - Droppings
     - Shelters

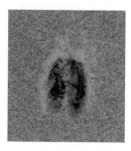

Photo of a deer track taken in Mr. Stock's driveway (February 6, 2013).

- Students must gather and hand in evidence of the presence of wildlife in their location (photographs, drawings, etc.). This evidence can be incorporated into the field notebook.

- Students must make a display consisting of a "field guide" to the wildlife in their chosen location. This display should consist of species descriptions for a minimum of four species of wildlife.

    o The attached page includes samples of species descriptions from wildlife in Yellowstone National Park. Students are familiar with the format of these descriptions, because we worked with them earlier this year. Student descriptions should be based mostly on what they observe. We may supplement with some additional information gained through research here at school.

expectation was that students would create knowledge from scratch and support it with evidence gained from their immediate surroundings. The results included images of woodchuck holes, hoof prints, deer beds, squirrels, birds, animal tracks of all kinds, and even archive photos of a bear that had wandered on to one student's property some time ago. Taken together, they offered a glimpse of our northeastern woodland ecosystem in the middle of winter.

As I reflect on the "trip" to Ellesmere Island and the Backyard Biology project that followed, many questions remain unanswered. To what extent had transformations taken place? If they had taken place, would they last? Would they be supported by additional experiences that would help my students to become "inhabitants of the scientist's world"? I don't have clear answers to these questions, but I do have an anecdote to relate.

Eight months after our trip to Ellesmere and three months after the Backyard Biology project, a student arrived in class sharing a digital photo of an animal carcass she had found near her driveway. What prompted her to do this? I don't know for sure, but this much I *can* say: She saw something in the natural world that caught her eye, and she made a conscious decision to document it. Then she chose to share her observations with others, and she knew exactly where to find an audience of colleagues who would be interested in reviewing her work. There's something very scientific about that, and I think a reasonable argument can be made that it's evidence of a transformation in progress.

Reading Our Way into an Ecosystem

So let's see where we are. We've just finished making observations and writing texts based on those observations. This seemed an opportune moment to show my students some writing by other authors who have done the same thing. The specific texts I used were species descriptions from an online publication of Yellowstone National Park titled *Yellowstone Resources and Issues Handbook* (see Figure 6). Before the Ellesmere trip, my students might have read such texts with some detachment, seeing only the words on the page. But the experience of making their own observations had provided them, as readers, with an image of what lay behind the words—scientists, much like themselves, sitting patiently in the wilderness with their eyes open and their pencils at the ready.

I presented students with descriptions of two different animal species, and I asked them to identify the design features the two texts had in common: headings, subheadings, images, copyrights, and bulleted lists of facts—features that commonly appear in nonfiction texts. I recorded this list on chart paper and then asked students to write a description of Arctic wolves using this format and these specific design features.

Figure 6. Species description from *Yellowstone Resources and Issues Handbook* (United States Dept. of the Interior 95).

Short-tailed Weasel (Ermine) (*Mustela erminea*)

©ZACHERY ZDINAK

Identification
- 8–13 inches long, 2.1–7 ounces.
- Typical weasel shape: very long body, short legs, pointed face, long tail.
- Males about 40% larger than females.
- Fur is light brown above and white below in summer; all white in winter except for tail, which is black-tipped all year.
- Compare to long-tailed weasel and marten.

Habitat
- Eat voles, shrews, deer mice, rabbits, rats, chipmunks, grasshoppers, and frogs.
- Found in willows and spruce forests.

Behavior
- Breed in early to mid-summer; 1 litter of 6–7 young per year.
- Can leap repeatedly three times their length.
- Will often move through and hunt in rodent burrows.

Why did I do this? I wanted my students to gain experience in presenting familiar information in a new way. I knew this would require them to develop an awareness of the expectations and constraints of this genre, knowledge that would serve them well as both readers and writers within the genre. It's also worth noting that this assignment dovetailed nicely with the CCSS (see RI.5.10 and W.5.2a). The writing standards for informational text make explicit reference to the grouping of related information, the inclusion of headings, and the use of illustrations to assist with comprehension. Quite frankly, this was a convenient opportunity to address those standards.

Once students had completed the writing assignment, we refocused on Yellowstone with the goal of using multiple species descriptions in combination to get at some important concepts and vocabulary in the discipline of biology. *The Yellowstone Resources and Issues Handbook* includes descriptions for many of the park's mammals. I printed these out from the park's website, cut them up, and dealt them out to each of the students. Some of the descriptions included images of the species, but others did not. Before they read the texts, I wanted to make sure that all of my students had a clear image of their species, so we went online. *North American Mammals*, a database operated by the Smithsonian Institution (www.mnh.si.edu/mna/main.cfm?lang=_en), had the images we were looking for. I showed students how to search this database for an image of their species, and I demonstrated how to copy, paste, and resize those images into a Word document. The final step was to label each image with the animal's common and scientific names and then print them out.

We began our reading of the Yellowstone species descriptions with a specific focus—to identify what each species eats. On a separate sheet of paper, students made a list of each food item consumed by their species. I asked them to highlight plant items in green and animal items in pink and to leave any remaining items unhighlighted. This involved some research—the use of dictionaries and Web-based resources—since many items in the descriptions were unfamiliar to my fifth graders (*forbs*, *sedges*, *carrion*, etc.). Then, with students working in teams of five, I asked them to sort their species into groups with "similar eating habits"—a sifting activity. As students developed and applied their criteria for membership in a group, the stage was set for a discussion that would either flush out some domain-specific vocabulary—*producer, consumer, predator, prey, herbivore, omnivore*, and *carnivore*—or provide an ideal opportunity to introduce it.

On the heels of this activity, I asked students to make a second food list—this time they had to list the animals that preyed upon their species. With the combined lists, each student had the information needed to begin our class project of generating a graphic representation of the feeding relationships in Yellowstone (see Figure 7). They used a segment of yarn to connect an image of their species to the things it eats and is eaten by. When the entire class had completed these connections, I asked my students to sit down in front of the display and describe what they saw. Some students reported seeing "a big web that [shows] what eats what"; others reported seeing "a lot of animals from Yellowstone park. There are herbavores, omevores, and carnavores. Also it show[s] what all the animals eat. The Bobcat and the Coyote eats the most." These students showed evidence of some understanding of a food web and a biological community. For other students, who reported seeing only "pictures, yarn, and tape," the transformation of vision had not yet taken place, and more transformative work remained to be done.

The concept of an ecosystem is critical to literacy in the discipline of biology. My approach to instruction was to build that concept from scratch by making observations, presenting those observations in writing, and reading a host of texts about a specific ecosystem in order to synthesize and make graphic representations of what we'd learned. This gave us a visual image of a biological community—interconnected and interdependent. And when we placed this community in the context of its nonliving surroundings—climate, rainfall, sunlight, etc.—we arrived at the concept of an ecosystem.

Figure 7. Food web produced by students as a graphic representation of feeding relationships in Yellowstone National Park.

Researching the History of Human Impact on Wolves

We began this journey by looking at wolves, a fixture of North American ecosystems since time immemorial. When Yellowstone National Park was created in 1872 by an act of Congress, the park had a large wolf population, but within seventy years they were gone. The maps in Figure 8 make it clear that this was not an isolated event—the disappearance of wolf populations happened on a national scale. And so I posed the following question to my students: "What happened to wolves in the lower 48 states between 1600 and 1973?" This question was more than just a topic for my students to ponder; it was the very point on which my instruction began to pivot. We were still on the topic of wolves, and everything we had learned about them as predators of large hoofed animals would help my students make sense of the history they would soon encounter. But a field trip to Ellesmere Island was now of limited value. Libraries, archives, and museums became more appropriate destinations.

In our curriculum, we were pivoting from ecosystems to westward expansion and human impact on the environment. In our disciplinary identities, we were pivoting from biology to history. And in our approach to constructing knowledge, we were pivoting from direct observation to historical research. I love this notion of pivoting, for it implies that we have one foot firmly planted beneath us as we turn to face a new challenge. Students and teachers who are pivoting don't have to spend much time orienting themselves to their surroundings. They know where they are and how they got there, and so they begin their next journey in familiar

Figure 8. Maps depicting the reduction in gray wolf range in the United States prior to the gray wolf's listing as an endangered species in 1974. From "Gray Wolf Range in the Contiguous United States" (United States Dept. of the Interior. Fish and Wildlife Service).

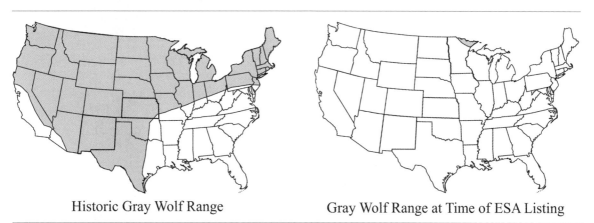

territory. There's a lot to be said for that. Furthermore, the juxtaposition of two different yet related tasks offers opportunities to link and distinguish between the kinds of literacy practices inherent in different disciplines. This is not the only way to transition from one unit to the next, but I would argue that it is a great asset to instruction.

We began our search for answers about the disappearance of wolves by reading excerpts from four different texts on the subject: Bobbie Kalman's *Endangered Wolves*; John E. Becker's *Gray Wolves*; Jill Bailey's *Grey Wolf*; and Stephen R. Swinburne's *Once a Wolf: How Wildlife Biologists Fought to Bring Back the Gray Wolf*. I demonstrated strategies for taking notes while reading, and students worked in pairs to read, discuss, and take notes on the texts. Before handing out the fourth and final text, *Once a Wolf*, I made a spur-of-the-moment decision to ask my students to predict what the text would say. This was, in many respects, a formative assessment of what they had learned from their reading of the previous three texts, and I was truly impressed with the results. They produced a list that included the following items:

- Europeans feared wolves.
- Hunters killed wolves' native prey, such as deer, elk, and bison.
- Wolves preyed on farmers' and ranchers' livestock.
- Farmers and ranchers killed wolves to protect their livestock.
- Wolves were trapped and poisoned.
- Bounty hunters killed wolves.

One of the most gratifying moments of our research project came when we read that fourth text. Every one of the items on the preceding list was actually in the text. Students had become so familiar with the discourse about wolves that they could successfully anticipate some of the content of a book on that subject. It makes me think of Ken Goodman's notion of reading as a "psycholinguistic guessing game." What helped these students to quickly become good guessers was the immersion experience of reading multiple texts on the same subject. This is what disciplinary specialists do all the time, and I think we can draw valuable lessons from this that directly impact the teaching of literacy in the disciplines.

What did we do next? We slapped and sifted the results of our research, much as we had done with our observations from Ellesmere Island. On strips of chart paper, pairs of students posted bits and pieces of information that could be used to answer the central question of our inquiry: *What happened to wolves?* I then posed the familiar question: "Do you see any items that seem like they belong together in a group?" Three categories emerged from the sifting that followed: habitat loss, wolves and livestock, and hired hunters. I left the category headings in place, but I removed the information that had contributed to their formation. Students then wrote their own narrative of what happened to wolves, addressing each of the three categories we had created and listing their sources at the end of the piece.

I want to take a moment here to reflect on the importance of the pivot that students made at the outset of this research project, the pivot from science to history. For starters, when my students delved into the history of wolves, they already knew something about the biology of wolves. This was very helpful. When they wrote about habitat loss, they understood the concept of a habitat, and they knew what it meant to lose it. Wolves need prey to survive, and if their native prey are in decline, they have two choices—find new prey or starve. My students also understood something of the farmers' and ranchers' perspective. They had watched a pack of wolves take down a musk ox, and they understood what wolves were capable of doing to cattle. The connection between the science and the history deepened their understanding of both.

The elimination of wolves from the Lower 48 is part of a larger story of the expansion of farming and ranching in the United States. The two things went hand in hand. Some view this history as the inevitable march of progress; others view it as a record of senseless destruction. Over the years, however, people on both sides of the debate have agreed on one thing—the government is a useful and powerful ally when it comes to managing wolf populations. And that point led us directly into our next inquiry.

The Politics of Wolves: How a Bill Becomes a Law

At the conclusion of our research project, my students knew that gray wolves had been hunted to the brink of extinction in the Lower 48. I took this opportunity to present them with a fair but challenging question: "Is there anything that can, or should, be done to prevent wolves from being completely wiped out?" This question marked yet another pivot point in my instruction.

Asking this question in certain parts of the United States could very well open up a contentious discussion. The majority of my students, however, do not live on farms or ranches, nor are there any wolves around to threaten the livelihoods of those that do. New York's wolves were hunted out long ago and they have not been reintroduced. So generally speaking, my students tend to fall on the "senseless destruction" side of the wolf debate.

I asked my students to write a response to my question and share it with a partner. The typical group discussion that follows has never failed to produce at least one suggestion that there should be a rule against killing wolves. Which begs the question: *Who has the power to make such a rule and apply it to all of the lower 48 states*? And that, my friends, is my introduction to our study of the United States government.

With this question, we pivot from the history of wolves to the future of wolves. We are no longer researching a problem; we are responding to it. To bring the forces of government to bear on the problem, students must understand how the government works—and we begin our investigation with the legislative branch. Time for a new identity and a new set of literacy practices. Public speaking, negotiation, and persuasion will factor heavily into this project.

I informed my students that they would be serving as legislators in the US House of Representatives. We went over the basic process for how a bill becomes a law, and then we dove right in to the process. So what does a bill need? The following five components:

- A description of the problem
- A statement of the bill's purpose
- A description of the powers the government has to address the problem
- A list of the prohibited acts
- A description of the penalties that will be given to those who break the law

Working with partners, students took strips of chart paper on which to record their best thinking about that first component—the nature of the problem. Before posting their ideas, I asked students to circle the one word or phrase from their writing that was most important to an understanding of the problem. This sifting produced the following list: *killing, decreasing, extinction,* and *wiped out*. The chart paper was then placed in a stack and reserved for future use by a congressional committee.

We did the same thing for the other four components of the bill. We had rich discussions on each of the topics, and the students generated a nice stack of chart paper representing the group's best thinking. The discussion surrounding the issue of penalties produced some interesting suggestions for punishments, including decapitation and a fine of up to a billion dollars. Let's just say the time was ripe for a discussion of the Eighth Amendment's prohibition of excessive fines and cruel and unusual punishments! I also took this opportunity to broach the subject of checks and balances, letting the students know that judges would have the power to strike down any part of their law that violated the Eighth Amendment. I didn't single out the work of any particular group, but I gave all groups an opportunity to revise their suggestions in light of this new information. I'm happy to report that the right people came forward and the appropriate revisions were made.

We then broke into five committees, one committee for each section of the bill. Each committee consisted of five people, and I asked one member to serve as the committee chair. I gave each committee the stack of ideas the class had already generated for use in each of their respective sections. Then I issued the following instructions: "Write your section of the bill. You can use the ideas the class came up with, or you can come up with your own. *You* have the final say on what goes into the first draft of the bill. A majority of the committee must approve the draft that you submit to me."

This last provision set the stage for one of my favorite moments in the congressional role-play activity. One committee was split on an issue, with two emphatic voices on one side of the debate and two on the other. The fifth member of the group was lying low. As the exchange continued, it dawned on the debaters that the silent member of the group held the deciding vote. Long story short, he could no longer remain a bystander. They began pitching their ideas directly to him with great passion, and they wouldn't take responses in the form of shrugged shoulders. His participation had become critical to the progress of the committee's work. The way in which they drew him into the debate was a thing of beauty. It was more effective than anything I could have done, and it was a perfect illustration of the legislative process in action.

As this anecdote suggests, the work of the committees occasionally ruffled some feathers, and I had to inform the class that their counterparts in the real House of Representatives shared those frustrations. It's the stuff of the evening news and the Sunday morning talk shows. By the time a draft of the bill finally came together, some battles had been won, others lost, and some compromises had been formed. The students' committee activity was, in fact, a lot like "real" life.

I formatted the bill and printed out a copy for each student. On *legal* paper, of course. Then I asked students to complete a comment form, indicating their intention to vote "yes" or "no" on the bill, as is. For those who liked the bill but wanted to improve on it, there was a third option—proposing an amendment to the bill.

The next phase of the process may ring a bell. It involved watching short video clips on CSPAN's website of actual floor debates in the House of Representatives. We took some mental notes on what people were wearing, and we picked up on some congressional lingo, including the standard line for ending a speech: "Thank you, Mr. Speaker. I yield back the balance of my time." This was all done to set the stage for a session of the House of Representatives to be held in my classroom, in formal attire, with a live audience of parents in the gallery.

On the day of the debate, students represented a state of their choice. We had a Speaker of the House, who led the entire session while I sat at the back of the room and watched. The session began with the strike of a gavel, followed by the Pledge of Allegiance. The legislators responded to the call of the Speaker—*The House will now recognize the gentlewoman from the state of Kentucky for two minutes*—and, one by one, students approached the podium to deliver their speeches.

Amendments were proposed and voted on. Changes were made. A vote was taken, and the bill passed with overwhelming support. A motion to adjourn was made and agreed to. And with a final strike of the gavel, the session came to an end, and a potluck lunch was served.

Some students described this event as one of the highlights of their year. What did I think? I enjoyed this culminating activity, but I was even more impressed by the work my students had done throughout the process of writing the bill. The degree to which their discourse echoed the actual historical discourse was striking. When my students passed their Wolf Conservation Act, they outlawed the killing of wolves. Congress did pretty much the same thing in 1973 by passing the Endangered Species Act—the piece of legislation that inspired this learning activity. The students' Wolf Conservation Act authorized the government to actively assist in the recovery of wolf populations by breeding wolves in captivity and reintroducing them to parts of their traditional range. Congress's Endangered Species Act created similar authority, and although captive breeding programs were not a part of the recovery plan for wolves, the technique was used to assist with the recovery of many other species, including bald eagles. As for a reintroduction of wolves to their historic range, that's exactly what the US government did in the mid-1990s.

My students also thought ahead to some of the details of reintroduction. They discussed the idea of purchasing cargo planes for the purpose of transporting wolves. They even went so far as to price them on the Web to determine how much money to put in their proposed budget. The planes were eventually cut from the final draft of their bill, but I found the discussion fascinating since, unbeknownst to them, cargo planes played a critical role in the return of wolves to Yellowstone National Park (McNamee). The overlap of the real and the imagined discourses was one of the wonderful outcomes of this activity. My students were speaking the language of species conservation, and I could prove that by citing evidence from both discourses.

Reintroducing Wolves: Back to Biology

By this point, my students had worn many hats, having served as biologists, historians, and legislators. As I congratulated them on their recent legislative achievement, I posed another series of pivotal questions that would prompt them to change hats once again: "Who will follow through on the things that are in your law? Who will operate the breeding facilities? Who will reintroduce wolves to Yellowstone?" And this is how I segued to our study of the executive branch. Having just emerged from the experience of writing legislation, the students pivoted one more time to embrace the new challenge of enforcing the law they had created.

With this final pivot, their journey came full circle. They reassumed their roles as biologists and reunited with an old friend from their Ellesmere Island days—Dave Mech, a wildlife biologist in the federal government and a significant player in the wolf reintroduction effort.

"Okay, biologists. If you're going to bring wolves back to Yellowstone, where are you going to get them from?" I asked. This is a writing assignment, a formative assessment to get a sense of their current thinking. Many suggest Canada—a logical choice, considering the observations of wolves they had made on Canadian soil earlier in the year. So now we're talking about Canada—a part of our social studies curriculum. It's the largest country in the Western Hemisphere and the second largest in the world. In other words, there are lots of places a biologist could go. Our task was to narrow down the options—and that means sifting. Our sieve would be constructed from what is known about wolves and the Yellowstone ecosystem: wolves need prey, most of their calories come from large hoofed animals, and the three largest populations of hoofed animals in the Yellowstone ecosystem are elk, bison, and mule deer, in that order.

Time to return to a familiar source of information—the *North American Mammals* database. Using range maps like Venn diagrams, the students set out to determine whether there are any places outside of Yellowstone where wolves, elk, bison, and mule deer can be found living together in the same ecosystem (see Figure 9). They analyzed the maps, identified sites that met the criteria, and marked their recommended capture locations by putting a digital push pin on a virtual globe in Google Earth. I instructed them to save these place marker files to a common location on the school's hard drive; I then uploaded the files to my own computer and projected the results for the whole group to see. With students' place markers displayed, I read an excerpt from a document published in 1994 by the US Fish and Wildlife Service as preparations for the reintroduction of wolves to Yellowstone entered the final stage.

> Wolves are a highly adaptive species and can utilize a wide variety of habitats and prey items. Wolves take[n] from almost any area of North America could learn, adapt, and thrive in the northern Rocky Mountains of the U.S. within a relatively short time frame (a few years or generations). A peer review of potential reintroduction techniques . . . indicated that the greatest opportunity for a successful reintroduction would occur if wild wolves, that were accustomed to preying on elk and deer in mountainous habitat (or possibly bison), were used for reintroduction. The best place to obtain wolves for reintroduction into the Yellowstone and central Idaho areas would likely be areas in the Rocky Mountains of Alberta and British Columbia (US Dept. of the Interior, *Reintroduction*).

Seven of my students had picked capture locations in the Canadian Rockies, mostly on the Alberta side. One of my students picked a location that was twenty-five

Figure 9. Maps students consulted to identify suitable ecosystems for capturing wolves for reintroduction into Yellowstone National Park. Sources include "*Cervus elaphus*: Elk," North American Mammals, accessed June 4, 2013, www.mnh.si.edu/mna/image_info.cfm?species_id=33; "*Odocoileus hemionus*: Mule Deer," North American Mammals, accessed June 4, 2013, www.mnh.si.edu/mna/image_info.cfm?species_id=229; "*Bison bison*: American Bison," North American Mammals, accessed June 4, 2013, www.mnh.si.edu/mna/image_info.cfm?species_id=23; and "*Canis lupus*: Gray Wolf," North American Mammals, accessed June 4, 2013, www.mnh.si.edu/mna/image_info.cfm?species_id=31.

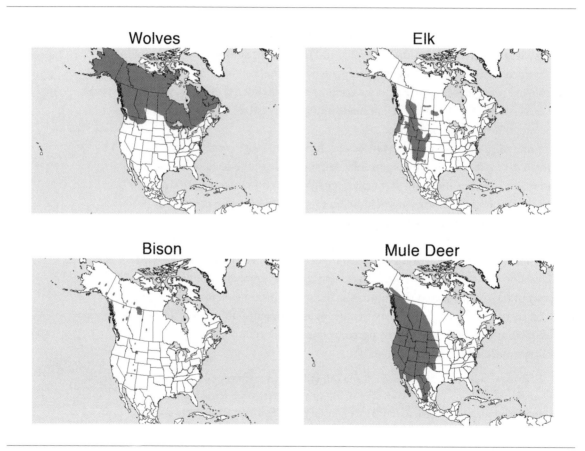

miles from the actual airport in Hinton, Alberta, where the first group of wolves destined for Yellowstone were put on a cargo plane and flown to the United States in 1995. The rest of my students picked locations elsewhere in Alberta and the neighboring province of Saskatchewan. A few chose to get wolves from the Rocky Mountains of northern Montana. All of the choices had ecosystems comparable to Yellowstone's.

Can we just barge into Canada and start taking wolves? Sounds like a good time to talk about the Canadian government. . . .

Final Thoughts

How do you prepare students to be inhabitants of a scientist's world, a historian's world, or a legislator's world? How do you prepare them to be creators of knowledge? Adopting some of the fundamental practices of the people who actually do the work of scientists, historians, and legislators in the real world seems like a good place to start. This is not something to be left for a later point in students' education. I feel it should *be* their education, from start to finish. The fact that tenth graders are currently struggling with the literacies of disciplines suggests that their involvement in those literacy practices needs to begin much sooner. As a fifth-grade teacher, I believe my students are ready for it. They are capable of observation. They can watch situations closely, record observations, discuss what they've seen with others, and present their thinking in writing. They can engage in the literacy practices of science, and the sooner they do so, the better off they will be.

Jeff Wilhelm has described inquiry as the rigorous apprenticeship into disciplinary ways of knowing (*Engaging*). This is what I strive to do . . . when I can. How I wish I had the time to do it more often. And oh, how I wish I knew how to do it better. I invite my students to play the roles of disciplinary specialists because I seek to create opportunities for them to grapple with real challenges and craft reasonable responses to them. This gives them a chance to experiment with a disciplinary way of *being* as they work their way toward a disciplinary way of *knowing*. And it is this transformative process that ultimately positions them to be inhabitants of the specialist's world.

Chapter Four
Spinning Revolutions and Creating History

Trace Schillinger

> *[D]isciplines represent unique languages and structures for thinking and acting; disciplines are spaces where students must encounter, be supported in, and be expected to demonstrate a plurality of literacies. This means taking a much more nuanced approach to disciplines and at the same time affirming the plurality of literacies.*
> —Literacies *of* Disciplines: An NCTE Policy Research Brief

In an eighth-grade humanities course that I regularly teach, a hybrid study of English and history, I invite my students to think about history very differently from how I was taught history: in this case, as a collection of important stories. I suggest they read historical documents and accounts in the same way they would read the novels they like. And when they take me up on my invitation, I find they connect both emotionally and imaginatively with the subject matter in the same way they connect with characters, events, and circumstances in novels that capture their interest and imagination. In the context of the humanities course, I am really inviting students to use the disciplinary practices they've developed in English studies—including reading, writing, speaking, and listening practices—as a set of tools to more fully explore the content of the history curriculum. To do this, I show them ways to approach reading their history assignments with the disciplinary practices they learned in their English studies in mind—that is, *how is language being used as a tool to provoke and express the imagination, to experiment with point of view, to bring the voices of historical figures to life?* In other words, I ask students to use these practices as tools for analyzing the perspectives of writers of history (and, by the way, for conducting the kinds of close readings called for in the Common Core State Standards [CCSS]). I also ask them to apply their knowledge of both content and craft to a variety of writing assignments that express their understanding of historical topics. In this way, I try to engage them in the disciplinary practices valued in the subject of history by asking them to draw on the literacy practices that are a part of their English studies.

At the center of my practice is this idea: beyond introducing students to the facts and terminologies of history, my goal is to help students read and write like historians. Research conducted around content area literacy instruction, like Shanahan and Shanahan's 2008 study, helped me to clarify my goals for literacy instruction in history:

> The historians . . . emphasized paying attention to the author or source when reading any text. That is, before reading, they would consider who the authors of the texts were and what their biases might be. Their purpose during the reading seemed to be to figure out what story a particular author wanted to tell; in other words, they were keenly aware that they were reading an interpretation of historical events and not "Truth." . . . History relies heavily on document analysis. These documents are collected after an event has occurred, and the selection and analysis of documents take place somewhat simultaneously. Thus, it is possible for a historian to choose and analyze evidence, unwittingly perhaps, that corroborates a previously held perspective. The historians we studied read with that caution in mind. Unfortunately, the nature of historiography (that is, how history is written and presented) is not often the subject of discussion in adolescent history classes. Students believe that they are reading to learn "the facts" and fail to take into account potential bias unless they are explicitly taught to do so. (11)

Because my school's mission is that education be transformational and inspire our students to participate in social justice endeavors, I bring this value into the history classroom. I ask students to question the many versions of and perspectives on historic events that we read. I ask them to think about how stories from the past that are often presented as "truth" are always only one version of many possible truths. We read remembering that authors who write history create the discipline's truths—its body of knowledge—as they frame stories from their angles of vision, which include their unique political, social, and economic identities and agenda.

A word about my school: Poughkeepsie Day School (PDS), an independent preK–12 school in the Hudson River Valley of New York, was founded during the Progressive Era and maintains a strong philosophical connection to John Dewey's democratic vision of education. Traditionally, PDS teachers offer courses in long blocks that engage students in the kinds of real-world learning that Dewey and William Kilpatrick argued for in the early 1900s. As a twenty-first-century secondary school teacher of English and history, influenced by Dewey's and Kilpatrick's thinking, I design courses to engage students in the practices, content knowledge, and projects that engage people who work outside of school in the fields I teach. In keeping with Dewey's and Kilpatrick's thinking, as I plan for my courses I try to connect my students' in-school studies to their beyond-school lives—both of which I think of as their "real worlds." As you'll recognize in the pages that follow, I also pay particular attention to how the learning activities I design align with the Common Core State Standards for English Language Arts & Literacy in History/Social Studies, Science, and Technical Subjects; the National Council of Teachers of English and International Reading Association Standards for the English Language Arts; and the National Council of Social Studies standards.

Teaching the Humanities in the Eighth Grade

The project I describe in this chapter is part of a humanities class in which I am responsible for teaching both ELA and social studies simultaneously and for which I am allotted a generous amount of time to work with my students, more time than many of us who teach only one discipline at a time experience. That said, the project I describe can be adapted to fit a variety of teaching contexts, either in single subject classrooms or team-taught or co-planned settings. And while no project will—nor should—look exactly like the one I describe here, adaptations created for other contexts can reflect principles like these that underlie NCTE's *Literacies of Disciplines* policy brief: students can come to understand and practice the literacies of disciplines by speaking, listening, reading, writing, and interacting like practitioners of those disciplines; literacies developed in one discipline (in this case, literary studies) can enhance learning in another (history).

When working with historical topics, I want my students to feel passionately connected to the past—to historical figures, events, and circumstances. And while I work to blend the subjects of English and history into hybrid form in my humanities course, I also work to honor the discrete disciplinary literacies of the two subjects, remembering Shanahan and Shanahan's (2008) assertion that "there are differences in how the disciplines create, disseminate, and evaluate knowledge, and these differences are instantiated in their use of language" (9).

In the humanities course, my goal is to combine subject English's focus on the literacy practices of imaginative literature, composition, and language studies to subject history's attention to the discourse of cause–effect relationships, critical analysis, and historical details. To my great delight, I've been able to use students' understanding of one to help inform the other. Although I have worked mostly as an English teacher, I love to study and teach history to secondary school students, in part because history is filled with interesting stories and challenging possibilities. As I mentioned earlier, this is not the way I was introduced to history; rather, much of my history education can be characterized by Joy Hakim's description of what happens in many secondary school history classes in which students are asked to read "tedious textbooks that are litanies of facts demanding memory and little thought" (12). Hakim says: "We bore kids, and teachers too, with routine teacher's guide exercises that allot only a small amount of time, if any, to probing the mind-stretching, intriguing questions that history asks" (13).

It wasn't until I began to teach history from my perspective as an English teacher that I learned to view history as the study of a series of stories, voices, and viewpoints to consider and analyze. Writing about the study of imaginative literature, Jeffrey Wilhelm captures the reasons why I love to teach history, particularly primary source documents:

> Literature is transcendent: it offers us possibilities; it takes us beyond space, time, and self; it questions the way the world is and offers possibilities for the way it could be. It offers a variety of views, visions, and voices that are so vital to a democracy. It is unique in the way it provides us with maps for exploring the human condition, with insights and perceptions into life, and with offerings for ways to be human in the world. ("*You Gotta*" 3)

In the English classroom, as we attend to how authors use language to compose versions of the truth—i.e., to the rhetorical choices they make—we examine how they create contexts, events, and characters with descriptions and word choices, and how they create roles and stances for readers to assume, or ways for readers to see and understand events portrayed or referenced. We talk about how readers read from the perspective of their unique understandings, how they attend to textual features that speak to them. In the humanities course, I ask students all year long to read history as they might read texts in the English classroom, to ask themselves and one another how the historians and historical documents we are reading add to our understandings, kindle our passions, and evoke emotional responses through their craft. Again, my aim when working in this manner is to encourage students to apply the literacy practices they acquire in their English studies to the discipline of history, to engage in interdisciplinary studies by means of literacy practices.

As the culminating unit in the specific humanities course I describe here, in what I called the Revolution Project, my aim was to help my students develop experiential understandings of American history and—as historians—to read and write history. I wanted them to create works reflecting their thinking about American history and contemporary America in which they used language in powerful and authentic ways—that is, to use language:

- To clarify their thinking about our topics of study
- To express their views
- To effect change; to provoke action
- To write passionately for clearly defined audiences and purposes
- To experiment with language; to express their ideas in clear, imaginative, fresh ways
- To play with ideas, develop their imaginations, and ignite their passion for our topics of study
- To question how the authors we studied over the course of the year, those who composed both primary and secondary source materials, might be writing to advance specific agendas or angles of vision and with a specific audience in mind
- To develop a spirit of skepticism by noticing and trying on for size a variety of voices, values, and ideas

When we began the Revolution Project in the spring, we had been practicing throughout the year the kinds of reading and writing I describe here, and students at that point were aware that readings and writings are rarely objective or neutral. When I asked students to bring the discipline-based practices we studied in English to the study of history, in effect I asked them to analyze how writers of history employed their craft to affect a readers' perspective on the subjects they were writing about. Throughout the school year, this type of work helped my students understand the literacy practices historians use to locate and interpret bias.

Preparing for the Revolution Project

The Revolution Project, the year-end unit, brought my eighth-grade humanities students back to one of the year's earlier topics, the American Revolution, and highlighted one of the year's overarching themes, social revolution. When studying various events in American history characterized as "revolutionary," we attempted to understand the forces at play behind events and persuasive people in the movements. We also attempted thematically to link the topics we studied. By devising a Revolution Project at year's end, I hoped my students might bring our year's thinking and learning about American history and revolutions to bear on contemporary American life.

Over the school year, I had engaged students in a variety of writing-to-learn activities similar to those I would ask of them in the Revolution Project. When studying the Salem Witch Trials, for example, I asked students to compose diary entries from the perspectives of several historical figures involved in these events. In their work, students imagined the hopes, influences, and concerns of these people based on what they were learning about them and the contexts in which they lived. To produce their diaries, students called on some of the rhetorical skills that are more often a part of English classes, spending time reading (or listening to) published diaries of well-known historical figures such as Anne Frank (1947) and Mary Chesnut (1905), studying these models as a way of coming to understand both the importance of the genre of diary as historical document and the rhetorical devices these authors used. At the end of the unit, students drafted a letter to the governor of Massachusetts, making specific recommendations to ensure that similar accusations and witch trials would not happen again. Students looked to real-world models, analyzing the published letters of famous Americans in terms of both content and writing strategies. Thus, my students used what are often thought of as English skills: writing imaginatively across several genres and studying the rhetorical components of those genres to enhance their understanding of historical events and concepts.

In other units as well, I encouraged students to call on the imaginative writing usually reserved for English classes. Several students wrote introductions to research papers as narrations of a scene they imagined, such as Pickett's charge or Frederick Douglass's escape from slavery. One student began a conventional research paper on the American Great Depression with a dialogue between a newly out-of-work father and his daughter before describing the causes and outcomes of this event. Others wrote persuasive letters from the perspective of imaginary people related to congressmen serving in the Second Continental Congress, attempting to articulate their specific concerns and persuade members of Congress to vote in particular ways on particular issues. To guide their efforts, students studied American documents of various genres, such as political pamphlets, political speeches, and even political posters and cartoons. These provided them with strong models for their own compositions. Students also engaged in a debate for which they had to prepare a series of documents (opening and closing statements, points and counterpoints, and decision papers) between the Taino people, Queen Isabella and King Ferdinand, and Christopher Columbus and his soldiers. And they engaged in a similarly structured debate as members of a community arguing the issue of teaching evolution versus creationism in schools.

What I describe might well be called a rhetorical approach to the study of history. To understand how people such as Thomas Jefferson, John F. Kennedy, Martin Luther King Jr. and the fictional Old Major from George Orwell's *Animal Farm* used language artfully to persuade others, we listened to a number of speeches and conducted close readings and comparisons of them, in the way we might read and compare literary texts. When we were analyzing political speeches, I asked students to notice common elements and patterns that speechwriters employed to generate powerful and persuasive documents. Based on these close readings and analyses, students discussed the emotional impact these rhetorical devices had on them as readers. From this work, we came up with a series of questions to use when examining a political speech or contrasting/comparing different views on a topic:

- What is the central situation addressed by the speech?
- Who is benefiting under the current situation?
- Who is suffering under the current situation?
- What is the call for action (what must be done)?
- What are some examples of use of literary devices?
- How does the author use
    - alliteration?
    - repetition of phrases or words?
    - metaphor to help listeners "envision" the meaning?
    - rhetorical questions—questions used for effect?
    - historical or literary allusions?
    - uniting language, such as a repetition of the pronoun *us* or *we*?

When my students and I studied contemporary slam poetry on YouTube, we were surprised to find these rhetorical elements at work in this genre as well. The connection between political speech and slam poetry excited the students who were fans of hip-hop and rap. Composing slam poems around current social concerns allowed us to practice using these rhetorical tools in engaging, original ways, again bridging the disciplines of history and English. We also noted these rhetorical figures as we read three speeches written on the topic of revolution at different times in history and for different purposes. We noted them in Frederick Douglass's "The Meaning of July 4th to the Negro," Elizabeth Cady Stanton's "Declaration of Rights and Sentiments," and Thomas Jefferson's "Declaration of Independence." Students also identified in each speech what we called "the language of revolution." From their underlinings and annotations of each speech, students created "found poems," in which they wove passages from all three documents into a poem for three voices, imagining that the three authors were speaking to one another about civil rights and revolution. Students performed these poems in groups of three so that we could hear the different voices. This proved to be a powerful exercise in summarizing the content of each speech, as historians would; in identifying how each author used language to evoke an emotional and persuasive response, and in analyzing the speeches for central common/contrasting themes, as literary critics would. It also allowed us to hear powerful, revolutionary language let loose in the classroom.

One of these poems illustrates one of the ways we used the literacy practices of English studies to explore the events and the discourse of history:

Jefferson: *Unalienable Rights*
Stanton: *the establishment of an absolute tyranny over her*
Douglass: *Do you mock me?*

Jefferson: *Happiness in life*
Stanton: *aggrieved, oppressed, and fraudulently deprived of their most sacred rights*
Douglass: *Disparity in fetters*

Jefferson: *Equality*
Stanton: *Unjust laws*
Douglass: *I am Not included*

Jefferson: *One people*
Stanton: *which belongs to them*
Douglass: *wanting respect*

Jefferson: *All men are created equal*
Stanton: *repeated injuries and usurpations on the part of man toward women*
Douglass: *This fourth of July is yours, not mine*

Jefferson: *alter their former Systems of Government*
Stanton: *immediate admission to all the rights and privileges which belong to them*
Douglass: *Your high independence only reveals the immeasurable distance between us*

—Nory, grade 8

The Revolution Project

By the time students engaged in the Revolution Project, they had a good deal of practice role-playing and using language to express and imagine different points of view on events in American history. Because I was going to ask them to role-play in the project, I began the unit by designing an activity that allowed us to talk explicitly about how viewpoints and perspectives shape people and events. I opened this activity by asking students to write to the following prompt:

> Write about a time when you felt defeated. This might be a moment when you were involved in something that made you feel embarrassed, ashamed, angry, humiliated, or sad.

This was private writing, so students did not share the content of their pieces. Instead, I next asked them to describe in writing how they felt when they were composing the piece and when they were reading it over. Students responded that they experienced negative emotions. Some said they felt upset, humiliated, hurt, "like it was happening again."

Then I asked students to rewrite the original scene and present it as a moment when they were victorious, using whatever literary devices they wanted, devices we had studied when working in the discipline of English. I asked students to present themselves in a positive light—to *spin the event*. Before writing, we considered how this might be accomplished. Students suggested that they might alter characterization, transform the setting, change the decisions that were made, include other characters, change the tone to a comic one, alter the plot by adding or deleting events, or write an explanation. Students knew this would be public writing, and they enjoyed sharing these pieces, which in general were humorous and positive. When I asked them to reflect on what it felt like to write and share this work, almost all said the work was fun and engaging. Seeing the negative event in a new light was an "empowering" exercise.

This revision, rewrite activity drew my students' attention not just to English and history studies' critical interest in perspective as a literacy practice, but also to the power of the author's perspective in historical accounts. It also helped me to prepare students for the roles I would next ask them to play. This activity enabled us as a "research" community to consider how a series of events that we documented—as we made and recorded history—might be portrayed in a variety of ways, depending on our perspectives and our agenda. In preparation for the Revolution Project, I explained to my students that we would be assuming roles that would allow us to investigate the function of perspective and agenda in the literacy practices of those who make history and then study the history they make.

From May through mid-June, my students experienced and studied how a modern-day group of American revolutionaries might attempt to enact radical change in the United States. I began the unit by distributing the following assignment to students:

Overview
We have been studying the concept of revolution this year. Now it's your turn to participate in one.

Task
You will be assigned to one of four groups:
- Revolutionaries
- Members of the president's Anti-Rebellion Task Force (a sub-branch of the Department of Homeland Security)
- A member of the media sympathetic to the revolutionaries
- A member of the media sympathetic to the status quo, anti-rebellion task force

You will consider, develop, and present your vision for a new America or the reasons to maintain the status quo in a variety of activities. Each group will receive an assignment sheet that will outline the exact parameters of your project. You will each receive a dossier, or folder of important documents, including the Declaration of Independence and the US Constitution. As you work, you may reference materials used throughout the year, including passages from a variety of primary source documents, and add historical allusions to events from American history as necessary.

My intention in asking students to reference documents we had studied earlier in the year was to help them make thematic connections and strengthen their familiarity with these works. In addition, these resources would serve as rhetorical models when I asked students to compose the documents they would need to produce during this unit. My more comprehensive goal was to help students understand that their Revolution Project work was to be informed by the thinking and writing of many people throughout history, people who were quite different from one another, but who dreamed similar dreams for their societies. As I developed the unit, I remembered historian Wilfred McClay's description of the "mystic chords of memory" that connect us to the past. McClay's idea of invisible threads of memory connecting humanity throughout time and space is evocative and poetic. By circling back to documents, events, and people we had studied, students might begin not just to understand the events themselves, but also to feel connections between themselves and the people they had studied. My hope was that students, in the context of their imaginative role-playing, would envision themselves picking up those invisible threads, see themselves among the historical figures they had studied. I wanted my students to learn history by taking on the roles of those who had created and recorded history.

I envisioned the Revolution Project as including a variety of public events—a rally, a song, a debate, a news conference, etc.—that I anticipated students would stage from the perspective of their particular groups in order to share and debate information and to negotiate. I was committed, though, to letting students decide what the events would be, what would best fit their given roles. I also realized that on occasion students would need to switch or add roles, not from one philosophic position to another, but to add the additional players that a particular event would require. (For example, if one of the media group members needed sympathetic members of a congressional committee to interview, members from their sympathetic media group would play those roles as well.)

Following each staged event, I asked students from both media groups (the "sympathetic to the revolutionaries" group and the "sympathetic to the status quo" group) to be responsible for writing accounts of the event so that we could examine how it was recorded from different perspectives and consider how historic events might be spun and dispersed, thus developing an understanding of some of the many ways history is made. For this endeavor to be successful, students would have to fully commit to their roles, as actors do in theatrical productions. I struggled over whether to let students choose their sides and their roles for this assignment, and though I could see the value in giving them the option to choose, after a year of working with the notion of multiple angles of vision, I decided to assign roles so that students could gain experience working with perspectives that might not come naturally to them.

Following are the assignments for each group:

> **You are a revolutionary.**
> As a group of revolutionaries: (1) you must choose your cause; (2) once you have chosen this cause, you need to draft a "manifesto" in which you outline your position and objectives; (3) you will clearly state the "crimes" committed by the US government; and you will then (4) declare your intentions for independence/revolution. You must use the Declaration of Independence, the Constitution, and any other historical documents we have studied to help illustrate your cause.
>
> **You are a member of the media sympathetic to the revolutionary movement.**
> It is your job to work with the revolutionaries to develop persuasive documents that will influence the American people to support their cause. However, remember that you serve as writers and editors, translating the intentions and concerns of the people interested in transforming the country. Often, the radical media comprises scholars, or "the intelligentsia." Your task is to produce (1) one op-ed piece; (2) an essay or pamphlet; and (3) a political cartoon.
>
> **You have been appointed to the president's Anti-rebellion Task Force, a sub-branch of Homeland Security. Two of you will represent the military.**
> The president has dedicated 500 million dollars to this task force. Your job is to find, identify, and suppress any potential rebellions on American soil, by whatever means necessary. You are guided by (but not limited to) the Constitution. Your task is to write a report to the president detailing all known data about the radical groups, including recommendations to suppress these groups, and recommendations about how to use this information as a platform for the upcoming election.
>
> **You are a member of the media sympathetic to the anti-revolutionary movement.**
> It is your job to work with the Anti-rebellion Task Force to develop persuasive arguments that will influence the American people to support the Department of Homeland Security. However, remember that you serve as writers and editors, translating the intentions and concerns of the president. Your task is to produce (1) a news story; (2) one op-ed piece; and (3) a public service announcement (print ad or video).

Once they received their assignments, students moved into groups and began strategizing.

At this point, my work was to assist students as they set goals for their individual groups, assigned roles to one another, and defined and organized their tasks. I also saw my job as helping to facilitate their group research endeavors by providing them with and helping them to locate resources they could lean on to accomplish their group's goals. Though this work occurred in a classroom context in which the message "you will complete this work" is always implied, I found myself subtly shifting my language use in ways that helped to reframe their roles from students to revolutionaries, authorities, or journalists. For example, rather than simply handing out assignments, I asked questions such as "How might we accomplish this goal?"; "How might your group solve this problem?"; "What needs to be done next?"; "How can I help you, and what do you need? "; "How might we solve this problem?" Questions such as these use the type of language that people in these positions and under these circumstances would genuinely ask one another. My goal was to promote a commitment to the task and ignite an intrinsic desire to accomplish a specific goal or pursue information.

Different groups had different workloads at different times depending on their tasks. I assigned readings that I thought might help: speeches, firsthand accounts, poetry, and songs from Zinn and Arnove's collection of primary source documents, *Voices of a People's History of the United States*, including Mary Elizabeth Lease's speech "Wall Street Owns the Country" (circa 1890); Mother Jones's "Agitation: The Greatest Factor for Progress" (March 24, 1903); e. e. cummings's "I sing of Olaf glad and big" (1931); and Bob Dylan's "George Jackson" (1971), to name a few. As they had throughout the year, students engaged in close readings of these primary texts so that they could apply both the content and the craft in the compositions they would generate throughout the unit.

The Revolutionaries spent the early hours of the project consulting various newspapers and Internet news sites to identify current issues that seemed front and center in national concerns. Emulating the primary source speeches they had read, the Revolutionaries composed the following statement of their concerns and then nominated one person to read it aloud—in a location they kept secret—to the group of media that was sympathetic to their cause:

> Who are we? We are the people. The workers, the ones who drive this country, and though we are not on the top of the feudal system of modern America, we are the foundation, and without us, this country would crack, crumble, and eventually fall to its defeat. It is time for revolution! It is time for a change. It is time for us, the working man and woman to break down the fences separating the rich and poor, to capture our dream, and for America to come together and give everyone a chance to succeed and a chance to accomplish what the founders of this country intended for

the citizens: Life, liberty, and the pursuit of happiness, for all, no matter what your background, belief system, or economic status. These are our inalienable rights.

Who are we? We are you! We are teachers, construction workers, janitors, police officers, people who work for minimum wage and people who work for more. We are Christians, Jews, Muslims, Hindus, mothers, fathers, friends. WE ARE AMERICA, the people, and not the government. We should have some say. The President works for us, not the corporations.

In America today, more that 12.5% of the population, that's about 35.9 million people, live below the poverty line, which is a minimum income level where a person is officially considered to lack adequate subsistence. These people are living in conditions so indescribably desperate, that a well-to-do person would not believe they were true. There is so much we want to achieve. The things we believe in are unquestionable and obviously just. This is our "Common Sense," this is what we will one day achieve:

- More access to medical care for everyone.
- More access to equal and competent public education, and less depending on the school's location to determine whether it is a proper place to learn.
- More jobs in the U.S. and less outsourcing.
- More rehabilitation centers and fewer jails.
- More youth centers and sex education classes in public schools, and less religion influencing how and what to teach children about the decisions they make in our public schools.
- More centers to help the poor get jobs and housing, and fewer shelters that only house people without really improving their chances of success.
- More freedom, more equality, less deprival.

Next, inspired by writers such as Thomas Paine and Frederick Douglass, this group of students reviewed pamphlets they had read earlier in the semester in order to apply the language and structure of these documents to their own pamphlets. The Revolutionaries distributed these pamphlets, which outlined their agenda to their middle school classmates. They also created posters and hung them on school walls. For students who did not know what was happening in my classroom, these posters and pamphlets became an exciting mystery.

Following these events, the group devoted to suppressing rebellion sprang into action. They held a special meeting during one class period to discuss the pamphlets being distributed by the Revolutionaries, as well as a copy of the speech that mysteriously showed up near their working spaces, and they strategized about reasons and how to suppress this group. Following their meeting, they decided to draft a letter to the president of the United States (a role taken on by another history teacher) in which they articulated the "threat." Again, students relied on the close readings and observational notes they had written as they studied historic letters and speeches throughout the year as they adapted various rhetorical moves to the tone and content of their letter:

> Dear Madame President,
>
> We have been informed of a group of rebellious individuals who identify themselves as working class individuals who have been stirring up trouble in recent days. These people are criticizing and demonstrating against our Country's educational and health care programs. At a demonstration last Tuesday, we were informed of the group's anti-capitalistic beliefs. They declared that there is an alarming gap between the wealthy and poor, and an evidently superior health care and educational opportunities for those from the upper class.
>
> In light of the upcoming election, we plan to handle this situation in a manner that will keep as many votes as possible, and we are worried that if these issues become central, we may lose the support of the middle class. We suggest figuring the greatness of this threat first. This would probably be achieved through a National poll. If the majority of Americans are content with the country's health care and educational system, we can ignore this group and make them look like maniacs and radicals. We can let the Country know that we are considering our own committees to look into inequity of health and education services. We can even say that we plan to establish several clinics and hire more teachers in the future. However, if most Americans support the goals of these revolutionaries, and believe that large changes must be made, that more money should be put into health and educational programs, we will have to address the issue with more force.
>
> Sincerely,
> The Anti-revolution Task Force (Branch of the Department of Homeland Security)

All of the students then participated in a series of events that required them to decide how each of their groups would act and react to fulfill their roles. My job at this point involved strategizing with each group separately to help them articulate the options available to them. Whenever possible I referenced strategies they had encountered in our history studies throughout the year. At other times, I provided current resources as examples of real versions of actions they were proposing and "to teach" them how to seek models for writing at other points in their lives. So my primary instructional role at this point was as co-researcher, co-learner, and advisor to each group. Throughout the process, I discovered there was much I didn't know about revolts in American history, and I too began to read and research. Although my students had a plethora of mentor texts available to them, as well as their own skill sets and knowledge developed throughout the year around close reading and writing in a variety of genres, I believe that observing their own teacher as learner taught my students even more about how learners approach studies and problems. And, as is often the case in teaching inquiry-based interdisciplinary projects, the pace at which students needed specific information to fulfill their tasks and move the action forward required my reading and research abilities, as well as my ability to distill the information I found into an appropriate construct for middle school.

Over the next two days, the Anti-revolutionary Task Force designed and conducted informal polls of middle school students and faculty during lunch and recess. They wanted to learn the extent to which their "society" might be sympathetic with the issues raised by the Revolutionaries. And they discovered that a large number of people in our school felt sympathetic to the Revolutionaries' causes. In light of this information, the group understood that they should take the Revolutionaries seriously. The poll results were made public for the class, and each news media group wrote articles in which they described the results of the poll. The group sympathetic to the status quo composed an article in which they promised to look into the issues in greater depth but questioned the polling methods and wondered if the results were flawed or distorted somehow. The group sympathetic to the Revolutionaries used the results to fuel the next staged event, a protest. The Revolutionaries took over the school's common room with picket signs. Both media groups wrote their version of the events. The media sympathetic to the Revolutionaries issued this news brief:

> **Is this America?**
> Today, May 31st, at 2:00 pm, a peaceful protest erupted into anarchy when policemen grabbed innocent protesters out of their organized, peaceful lines and arrested them for no good reason. As one protester stated, "We were being peaceful, stating our views. Then a policeman comes and arrests my friend right out of nowhere." The feelings of this one, disgruntled protester reflect those of many. All Americans are aghast at this violent turn of events.
>
> Before the protest began, this group of Americans who identify themselves as mostly "working class," were insulted by the government, because they downplayed the results of a National poll that seemed to call for dramatic social reform, because of the inequities of opportunities offered to the rich and everyone else. Now that the government has arrested people without cause, everyone has a reason to be scared. They are ignoring The Constitution and our First-Amendment rights. Protesting the inequality coming from the current Presidential administration, this group of revolutionaries is disgusted with how the money-ruled government would not support the working class.
>
> You can't get a good job without proper education," said Emma Weinstein, the leader of the revolutionary group. "However, the only way to get a good education is to go to college, which is becoming almost impossible for many working middle class Americans. And it's easy to see, especially now, how things have changed from our American dream. The government is denying us the basic human rights that our

founding fathers fought and died for." The rally began with a rousing verse of "We Shall Overcome," and everything was calm. However, just as soon as Weinstein began her speech, police stormed the building, arresting many of the protestors. No longer is the government sitting by, that's for sure. They're so worried about keeping the money to themselves and giving the rich all kinds of benefits, that they have begun breaking civil liberties. It will not be long, now, before they go full out and start enslaving people again.

The media sympathetic to the Anti-rebellion Task Force wrote their version of the protest:

> **Sadly Organized, Off-tune Choir Dub themselves "Revolutionaries"**
> Late yesterday afternoon, a group of changing cultists provoked boos and laughter, during their "demonstration." They began this "demonstration" with an attempted singing of, or rather, maimed version of "We Shall Overcome," which caused much amusement among passers by. The group criticized many modern day values and degraded the foundation of America's society, by calling it "tiny green sheets of paper." The supposed "demonstration" did not last long before falling into a sad state of chaos, which provoked more laughter and caused many bystanders to leave in disgust. It soon became apparent that many of these supposed "revolutionaries" were embarrassed, which they exhibited by blushing furiously and shamefully covering their faces with their "pamphlets." These handouts and the accompanying protest signs displayed a fist, greedily clenching money. It is very interesting that they chose this symbol to represent them, because they never clearly explained its significance throughout the entirety of their speech. Their "revolutionary leader" spoke about money as an idea and how our culture is based on a fight for it, but had very few accurate facts and figures to back up her assertions. Halfway through their "demonstration," things began to get a little violent. Our reporters witnessed brutal violence committed by the "revolutionary leader" on other members of the group. This highly dangerous tone of the protest caused members of the police to arrest certain individuals. It is the general belief that there was more than today's violence contributing to reasons for their arrest, however. It is believed that there may be a criminal element involved here. President Holdsworth plans to make a statement to the press in response to this sad demonstration. We will cover her address at a later date.

Prepared by the Anti-revolutionary Task Force and press sympathetic to it, a faculty member, Geetha Holdsworth, acted as president and gave a press conference that was covered by both media groups. She read a speech prepared by the task force and answered questions from both sides after being "briefed" by the task force.

The media affiliated with the Revolutionaries wrote the following piece after the president's speech:

Leaders Take Revolutionaries Seriously: A Presidential Press Conference
During an emergency press conference at the White House, President Geetha Holdsworth found it necessary to remind those attending that we were in America. She seemed to wash her hands of the labor disputes encouraged by the revolutionaries, when she asked the rhetorical question, "Are you really speaking for all America? How do you know?" President Holdsworth also clearly stated that since America has so many economic interests and enemies abroad, she does not want to worry about domestic issues. President Holdsworth was also kind enough to tell us once again that we were in America, where presumably, "No one is denied health care." Many Americans feel that those words are far from the truth.

President Holdsworth asserted that it is up to the individual to improve their own financial situation. She cited several famous Americans who have overcome adversity and led successful lives. Holdsworth also asserted that the Federal Government does not create jobs, rich corporations do. (What does it mean though if the Government arrests people for protesting—a Constitutionally protected right—protesting against greed. Are they the police for the corporations?). An unnamed source in the press room said that Holdsworth's unsympathetic and biased response to the protestors will encourage the revolutionaries to use their influence to encourage an eruption of union strikes. Upon hearing this, President Holdsworth responded that, "The President can break strikes if necessary." Historically though, the breaking of strikes is rare and is usually justified if the President feels that the strikes threaten national security. It will be fascinating to see what happens. One disturbing reminder of the arrests and abuse of power by the government was apparent in the pressroom, because the man who led the arrests was sitting happily near the President.

The media supporting President Holdsworth's position wrote this:

A Presidential Press Conference
USA: One Nation for All
Today we will provide you readers with an inside look at the touching speech made by the President in an address to the Nation about issues which have been taken up by a group of protesters who call themselves (so called) "revolutionaries."

Last night, President Geetha Holdsworth made a speech addressing the conflicts many "revolutionaries" had brought up during their protest. She touched the hearts of many Americans and took an in-depth look at what is really important in life, and in the eyes of true Americans. She was asked questions regarding her healthcare policy, her money released to schools, poverty levels, and more.

Some members of the press tried to get Holdsworth to address the issue of the number of people below the poverty level. Holdsworth responded by stating, "Poverty is mainly a result of undocumented entrances into the USA. . . that is a security problem." Holdsworth clearly stated that she believes that these so called, "revolutionaries" are simply raising petty problems that only these extremists think are really important. This may be a liberal tactic to increase her criticism before the upcoming election. Holdsworth asserted that people are able to relieve themselves from poverty if they have faith in the government and work hard to make money for themselves. We must remember that if corporations are not given governmental support, jobs cannot be created, and people cannot become wealthier. Sound economic theory. But what was most touching about Holdsworth's speech was the word of hopeful advice that our President gave to people who may be living in circumstances they would like to change: "If you put in the blood, sweat, and tears, you can rise above any circumstances. Think of our founding fathers. Think of Frederick Douglass. Think of Abraham Lincoln. Think of the suffragists fighting for the rights of women!"

While the radicals think it may be time for a social revolution in this country, many people are of the opinion that they are being greedy and selfish and not thinking these issues through. Is a revolution safe for America? Do we need to have domestic enemies as well as foreign ones? And the answer is "NO!" Why start a revolution now, when America is just trying to make the world a peaceful place? Do these "revolutionaries" want to ruin the country? What are they really planning on doing? Making us all communists? President Holdsworth is protecting us and our "natural rights." She has looked into every issue, and this time, the extremists have gone too far and they don't have their facts straight! Together, with the guidance of our wise President, we can keep this United America abounding.

Tactics

Since they had received the attention of the government and the president herself was responding to them and their issues, the Revolutionaries decided they needed to do something dramatic to be taken seriously by the government and move their agenda to the next level. Encouraged by the poll results that led the entire class to believe they had some valid ideas, the Revolutionaries decided to create an opportunity that would take their ideas to Congress, where they might most successfully effect change.

Because our eighth-grade Revolutionaries imagined that their group had gained significant attention and influence, they believed they would be able to garner support from workers and their labor unions. This seemed like an ingenious idea to me. We had studied workers' unions only briefly over the course of the year (and, in hindsight, I wish we had given more attention to this topic), but once the Revolutionaries latched onto the idea, they were able to research and locate precedent for this sort of action. This moment in the project illustrated the powerful fact that when students committed fully to their imagined identities, the project began to follow its own logical course, one that emerged out of the students' work and interests. At this moment, the project took on a life of its own, one that was difficult to predict when planning months in advance. In a learning situation like this, I'm convinced that it's crucial that teachers be flexible and willing to follow students' leads, while making sure that students are gaining content knowledge and developing disciplinary and general academic skills.

So how can we do this? How can we teachers give students room—once they have committed themselves to their roles—to become, in the case of my students, history makers and historians? What does teaching look like in a project that engages students in the roles of practitioners of the literacies of disciplines? A familiar formulation comes to mind: coaching. But coaching isn't the whole story. Certainly, in this kind of inquiry-based, project method instruction we teachers coach our students to successful enactments of their learning, but the key phrase here is *their learning*. Coaching often implies that I guide students in learning how to successfully execute already developed learning that I've introduced to them or helped them to understand. I do that, to be sure, but I do something else as well. As my students are developing new learning about revolution, a fundamental topic in American history, their learning is emerging from their interdisciplinary study of American history, history makers, the historians who have told their stories, and the literary study of storytelling. I work to support *their learning* as a consultant might, as one who's done this work before and might guide a new constructive approach to it. I pose questions, offer advice, and, most important, direct students to materials that are relevant, accessible, and age appropriate. These actions define what I believe is the crucial role of my work as a teacher at this moment in the project. With my help, students located several examples of large-scale American strikes or threats of strike from railroad workers, airline workers, and miners. One student even discovered that there had been a plan during the beginning of World War I for international unions to oppose their governments in an effort to stop war.

In response, however, the Anti-revolutionary Task Force learned that other presidents over the course of US history had worked with management or even invoked executive privilege and used the military to stop strikes. This strategy came from a dinner table conversation one student had with his parents. Once the strategy was articulated, it was my job to lead my students in researching similar events. With my support, students in this group were able to cite the ways in which presidents such as Theodore Roosevelt, FDR, and Ronald Reagan had dealt with labor strikes. This group also debunked the Revolutionaries' idealistic vision of international labor unions working to end war by asserting that in the end, the World War I–era strikers ultimately backed down and supported their governments.

Negotiations

As students prepared for, staged, and then wrote their "spin" pieces in response to a series of events they conducted, they also honed in on how the two opposing groups might find some sort of compromise. The Revolutionaries imagined that their influence had grown significantly, and that they had enough power to encourage unions to threaten to go on strike unless Congress agreed to consider four proposals to be written as bills that would address what the group identified as its major demands. The students who worked to oppose the Revolutionaries asserted that if the rebels were able to influence union strikes, the president would break the strikes and possibly take military action, invoking executive privilege. Both scenarios seemed devastating, so, with my encouragement, both groups decided to face off in a debate during a congressional session in an attempt to compromise over the four points. The Revolutionaries convinced one member of the Anti-revolutionary Task Force to draft four proposals and put them up for congressional debate and vote.

Proposal One reflected the Revolutionaries' concerns about inequity in our national education system. Students read a variety of articles on this topic, such as William H. Schmidt's "Inequality in the American Education System," which can be found on Huffington Post.com, and passages from Jonathan Kozol's book *Savage Inequalities: Children in America's Schools*, and were distressed to learn that schools are largely funded by taxes collected in the neighborhoods where schools are located. The students concluded that if states collected school taxes and distributed them equally, this might help to address the problem.

Proposal Two addressed the discrepancies students perceived in health care in our nation. Again, they were distressed to learn from readings such as a report out of Baylor University Medical Center (Mayberry, Nicewander, Qin, and Ballard) and on sites such as Wikipedia (http://en.wikipedia.org/wiki/Health_equity) that many people, including children, do not have health care coverage because they can't afford it, while people who are financially well off have access to high-quality hospitals, doctors, tests, and services. The students described a national health care program modeled after their (cursory) understanding of programs in Europe. Their second proposal required Congress to address the practices of insurance companies and to set aside funds to offer the same health care services to all Americans, regardless of income.

Proposal Three was a response to students' reading that cities and corporations often set up power plants or dispose of toxic chemicals in residential neighborhoods, most often underserviced and underrepresented neighborhoods, where people are unable to resist these dangerous impositions. Students' thinking was shaped by articles published in the *New York Times*[1] such as "Battling Dumpsites in Poor Neighborhoods" (Tuhus, June 30, 1996) and "Pollution's Chief Victims: The Poor" (Kennedy and Rivera, August 15, 1992), as well as excerpts from Jonathon Kozol's *Amazing Grace* (1995). The group felt that Congress should pass legislation to educate citizens about these health hazards and to make municipalities and corporations take responsibility for the toxins they force into these spaces.

Proposal Four was written in response to students' reading about the dire conditions of hospitals serving residents in underserved and underrepresented neighborhoods. Students learned about this topic from works such as Kozol's *Amazing Grace*; Jim Yardley's *New York Times* article "A City Struggles to Provide Health Care Pledged by U.S." (August 7, 2001); and Jane Gordon's article "At Hospitals, a Cushion for the Poor," also published in the *New York Times* (June 8, 2003). Students imagined that the federal government could allocate funds to help these hospitals improve their level of care so that people who needed their services could be offered high-quality health care.

Before the congressional debate, the Revolutionaries and media sympathetic to them located and were provided with readings that presented a variety of perspectives on, and offered a variety of solutions to, the problems the Revolutionaries raised. Again, it was my job to serve as a consultant, strategist, and researcher. Based on their interests, I located readings that provided students with content and mentor texts to guide their work. The readings focused on the discrepancies between health and educational services provided in rich and in poor neighborhoods, the problem of a shrinking middle class, and corporate focus on profits. The texts included Emily Eakin's *New York Times* article "On the Dark Side of Democracy" (January 31, 2004) and Ray Boshara's *New York Times* article "Poverty Is More Than a Matter of Income" (September 29, 2002).

As the teacher, I supported the Anti-Revolutionaries and the media sympathetic to them in the same way I supported their opposition, so these groups were given and they found texts that examined the same issues, primarily health care and education, focusing on the complexities in solving them. These articles cited examples of individuals who worked to escape poverty and of individuals who solved the identified problems in ways that did not require significant financial support from the government. Students read essays and interviews of community activists in publications such as *Magpie: Who's Changing My Hood?* and *About Face: Portraits of Activism*, published by the Student Press Initiative; Paul Tough's *New York Times* article "The Harlem Project" (June 20, 2004); Greg Winter's *New York Times* article "Long after Brown v. Board of Education, Sides Switch" (May 16, 2004); and Barack Obama's "Remarks to the Democratic National Convention," published in the *New York Times* (July 27, 2004). These groups also read articles focusing on American corporations' challenge to create and provide jobs in a global economy, such as Chris Isidore's "Economists Mixed on Kerry Plan: Conservatives Applaud Cut in Corporate Taxes, but Even Liberals Doubt It Would Stop Outsourcing" (CNN News, March 26, 2004), and on the demands of the federal budget to fund overseas military endeavors in the name of national security, such as "Democrats in Debate Clash over Iraq War" written by Adam Nagourney and Diane Cardwell (October 27, 2003).

A Final Debate

Both media groups reported on the congressional debate. The following article was written by the media sympathetic to the Revolutionaries:

> **A Victory in Congress: Bills Will Be Considered**
> Today, in a meeting between the President's Task Force and the revolutionaries, an agreement was reached. After painstaking weeks of planning and hours of debate in Congress, the revolutionaries were able to, after threatening with a hefty list of unions that backed them up, influence Congress to deliberate and vote on two proposals that will pave the way for social reform. The first proposal states that all American neighborhoods with proven health hazards will be offered services, such as proper testing of the hazardous sites, medical care for those at risk, especially children, and educational programs on all related issues for the inhabitants. The other proposal will increase federal contributions to publicly funded hospitals, especially those that relocate to under-served, urban areas where people living below the poverty level reside. Both proposals offer services that are very important to the working class today. Although this is clearly a great victory, this "war" on workers' rights is far from over. There is much left to do.

And this article was written by the media sympathetic to the status quo:

> **Face Off: Government Proves Reasonable and Sympathetic to Those in Need**
> A head to head debate between members of the radical group, "the Revolutionaries" and the government occurred today in Congress. Leaders of the revolutionary group brought their issues forward and negotiated with the government. One government official noted, "There were many flaws found within the argument on the side of the extremists. While speaking, one of the members happened to quote the wrong American document. When put under pressure, the radical side was irrational and extremely unorganized. Reduced to chaos, the revolutionaries continued to cut each other off in the middle of their sentences, and yell over the top of each other's voices. As things were getting out of hand, one even picked up The Constitution of the United States, and threw it on the ground. The Constitution. On the ground. The document that this country is based on, that these revolutionaries are trying to use to support the "rights" they claim are being denied, rights set down by our founding fathers, and yet they can't help to even take care of this sacred document.
>
> Overall, these rebels were constantly rambling and harshly verbally abusive toward the representatives of the Federal Government. By throwing The Constitution, one of the most treasured American documents, these people are now considered a disgrace to their country.

In the end, the government always pulls through, and they managed to compromise, agreeing to deliberate and vote on proposals three and four, while proposals one and two were clearly impossible, and incredibly ridiculous propositions. Of course the issues raised in proposals three and four were issues that Congress was planning to address anyhow.

Proposals Three and Four, smaller in scope and a bit easier for the groups to deal with, were passed. The Revolutionaries got half of what they asked for. Students learned that if you are willing to give something, you might just gain something as well. Proposals One and Two, though well argued, seemed too complex to resolve in our eighth-grade classroom (as in real life). The Revolutionaries told their union supporters to back down and vowed to spend their efforts "watching" the government to make sure it fulfilled its promises. They also determined to reassemble and find other ways to work on the issues raised in the first two proposals.

Although the Revolutionaries raised some important issues for their society to consider and debate, students wondered if they had really participated in a social revolution, or if they had simply raised awareness about issues, begun a debate, and initiated some minor changes. All the same, they concluded that theirs was a pretty significant accomplishment on many levels.

On reflection, it seems to me that one significant accomplishment in this work was that students not only were afforded the opportunity to contemplate the issues that arose in this project and develop and refine their rhetorical skills, but they were also invited to solve a series of real-world problems that the historical figures whom they had met in their American history studies also struggled with. They were invited to solve problems rather than merely study how others have attempted to solve similar problems in the past. These students, by virtue of their role-playing, were able to wrestle with these challenges within the safety of their classroom, their assigned roles, and the spaces of the disciplinary communities of history and English. My hope is that students will be able to translate what they learned during this project into what Nobel Laureate Herbert Simon described as identifying and using knowledge to address similar problems that might arise in the future. If so, I believe that taking on roles of actual practitioners in the disciplines of English studies and history was a rehearsal for whatever real-world challenges arise.

A few years after I taught the Revolution Project described here, as the Occupy movements across our country have receded into the landscape, I remember what my eighth graders and I learned about American history and the role revolution has played in it: Social change takes a lot of work and compromise. It is almost impossible for a revolution to take hold. Maybe that is why successful revolutions are so rare. Maybe that is why they are called revolutions. Maybe those that succeed do so because the causes that inspire them are broadly embraced by the society in which they take shape.

Note

    1. At PDS we subscribe to the *New York Times*. For this project, I copied articles for students to read. The following resource is now available for teachers and their students online: www.nytimes.com/subscriptions/edu/lp2266.html. I also pulled articles from online resources such as CNN Student News: www.cnn.com/studentnews/index.html.

Chapter Five
Learning for and with Our Students

In a remarkable essay on "how does one make a revolution?," the physicist W. Heisenberg puzzled his readers with the unexpected answer: "By wishing to change as little as possible." Heisenberg justified this unexpected answer by recounting the history of physics and demonstrating that radical changes of thought patterns in the history of science have come about through those who genuinely tried to solve "special, narrowly restricted" problems but who otherwise wished to change as little as possible in the previously existing physics.
—Heath, "The Education of a Teacher"

As you begin reading this last chapter of our book, we're thinking that Trace's Revolution Project is fresh in your mind. In keeping with the theme of that project, we've opened this chapter with a note about revolution—not about revolution to change the shape of a society, but about revolution to change the direction of thought in a field of knowledge. The passage describing Heisenberg's account of change of thought patterns in science was written by the linguistic anthropologist Shirley Brice Heath in a preconference paper she shared with a group of educators who were considering how teacher preparation programs might be beneficially reformed. The conference met amid calls for the reform of teacher education that emerged across the 1980s from within and beyond our profession. Heath cited the

Nobel Prize–winning physicist in preparation for the recommendation she made in her paper that we paraphrase this way: if we are to change teacher preparation beneficially, we should concentrate efforts on preparing and making it possible for teachers to be learners for and with their students.

Of course, the change Heath recommended to improve teacher education was grounded in changes for which others had called before. Think of the changes we mentioned earlier that John Dewey and William Kilpatrick identified and recommended when they called for teachers to position students as inquirers who play active roles in the construction of knowledge. And think of the changes that workers in the Writing Across the Curriculum movement identified and addressed when they circulated in professional development settings countless activities—like those Patti describes in Chapter 2—that teachers might use to engage students in the development of subject matter knowledge. And think of the changes the teacher research movement, widely encouraged in teacher preparation programs since the 1980s, identified and addressed when it demonstrated the many ways that teachers can inquire into their teaching and their students' learning for the benefit of both.

Whether we think of these teacher-led reform movements as separate strands of work designed to beneficially change teacher education or as constituent parts of the one change for which Heath called, they came together to benefit our teacher preparation and, we imagine, yours as well. Our teacher education introduced us to social constructivist theories of learning, the centrality of literacy to learning, "kid watching," and more. We were prepared to be learners for and with our students.

Paradoxically, the teacher education that prepared us to teach inquiry-based interdisciplinary projects like those illustrated in this book is too seldom put into practice in schools. NCTE's *Literacies* of *Disciplines* policy brief reminds us why: "[S]chool subjects often operate to constrain or control how knowledge is presented, while disciplines emphasize the creation of knowledge" (1). While the good news is that we teachers have been prepared to design and offer instruction that will engage our students in creating knowledge and in learning the literacies of the disciplines that created the subject matter they are asked to learn, the less happy news is that for too long the organization of school subjects has discouraged such instruction. Optimists that we are, however, we hope that a silver lining of the CCSS—which give literacies of disciplines a central position—will make increasingly possible the kind of teaching that the 1980s research-supported reforms of teacher education programs prepared us to offer.

As this book illustrates, when on-the-ground policy permits we engage our students in inquiry-based interdisciplinary projects that not only position them as active learners of subject matter and of the literacies of the disciplines that produced that subject matter, but that also position *us* as students of our students' learning, which can only benefit that learning. In this chapter, referring to the inquiry-based interdisciplinary projects we've shared with you, we want to talk about two of the numerous sets of activities in which we continue to work to be learners for and with our students. First, in a discussion of formative assessment, we focus on how we work to be learners for our students by being learners with them. Then, in a discussion of professional learning communities (PLCs)—in their most generative forms—we focus on how we work to be learners for our students by being learners with our colleagues.

Formative Assessment: Learning with Our Students

As you've seen, we engage in considerable study to draw up the road maps to preparing instructional materials for the units of study we teach, attending to local and state requirements and to scholarship in our fields that our instruction must address. We also continually engage in formative assessment of our students' learning and adjust our day-to-day teaching in light of our students' needs. That is, we shape our day-to-day teaching to take advantage of students' insights, to address their questions, to give language to the confusion we see in their eyes, to take next steps when they are ready and to step back when retraced steps are called for. It is not too much to say that just as subject matter and the discipline-based literacy practices that produce it are reciprocally related in the inquiry-based interdisciplinary projects we teach, so too are instruction and formative assessment of our students' learning.

NCTE's *Literacies* of *Disciplines* policy brief puts our point this way: "Classrooms where literacies of disciplines flourish are nurturing environments for formative assessment. . . . Teachers can use formative assessment to shape instruction based on student progress; considering student performance enables teachers to pinpoint areas where students may need more focused teaching" (2). As learners for and with our students, formative assessment is a continuous process in our classrooms—a process that not only pinpoints areas where students need more focused teaching, but also offers opportunities for review and reinforcement of learning, signals where originally unplanned instruction should be brought to bear, and sometimes even serves as summative assessment (see Figure 10). With specific reference to Andrew's Wolf Project, we want to illustrate these multiple, beneficial functions that formative assessment plays in our classrooms. Throughout Chapter 3, Andrew draws our attention to examples of the reciprocal roles that formative assessment and instruction play in the Wolf Project. For example, in his account of his first assessment of students' learning about the wolves of Ellesmere Island, Andrew describes his intention for the activity to serve two purposes: (1) he wanted his students to demonstrate in writing what they had learned up to that point about the subject matter they were studying, and (2) he wanted the strengths and weaknesses of his students' organization and discussion of that information to inform the devlopment of his up-coming writing instruction. Pointing to this overlap, Andrew tells us that he prepared students for this assessment by asking them to review and think as practicing wildlife biologists would about what they had learned so far about wolves. Specifically, he asked them to work with a partner to record observations about wolves that they made individually in their field notebooks. Then, in an "observation slap," he asked them to share their observations with the whole class. With the facts and scope of their observations on display before them, he asked students to sort their observations into categories. In effect, as the fifth graders talked, wrote, viewed, manipulated, and mulled over the information they'd gathered about wolves, they studied and organized it as the auditory, visual, kinesthetic learners they are, and in so doing prepared themselves to write about what they had learned.

When Andrew asked students to write a description of the wolves of Ellesmere Island and to include in their description a section for each of the categories they had developed, he left their categories—but not the observations they assigned to those categories—in full view as they wrote. While this first essay of the project allowed Andrew to evaluate what each student had learned about the wolves on Ellesmere Island, it also served as a formative assessment of their abilities to compose a text with sections devoted to categories of information. Andrew studied this formative assessment to determine how he would shape the upcoming writing instruction he was planning for the class.

Another example of the reciprocity of formative assessment and instruction that Andrew describes in Chapter 3 allows us to identify one of the most generative lessons students learn when they engage in inquiry-based interdisciplinary projects, a lesson that evades measurement in tests designed for general use across

Figure 10. Formative assessment and instruction in Andrew's inquiry-based interdisciplinary classroom.

- Pinpoints areas where students need additional teaching
- Offers opportunities for review and reinforcement
- Leads to new approaches to instruction
- Is both teacher-led and student-led
- At times does double duty as summative assessment

classes, schools, and school districts. You'll recall that after their Ellesmere Island virtual field trip and the work students did with the information they gathered on it, Andrew asked them if they felt like wildlife biologists. Because they'd been enthusiastically engaged in their learning and had produced essays demonstrating that they had learned a great deal about wolves and about how biologists think, talk, and write about wolves, Andrew was surprised when a number of his students indicated they did not feel themselves to be wildlife biologists. They explained that their observations had been of wolves in videotaped settings and activities, not in the wild. Responding to the opening his students provided and taking advantage of their enthusiasm for wildlife observations they might make "in the wild," Andrew developed the Backyard Biology Project that positioned his students as observers of wildlife in their home environments, where they could be on-site wildlife observers. Again, a formative assessment—this time simply asking his students about their learning—led to instructional change.

While the Backyard Biology Project is a clear example of how formative assessment works in "classrooms where literacies of disciplines flourish," we want to draw attention to the student learning that prompted it. Most often the value of formative assessment is described as enabling teachers to "pinpoint areas where students may need more focused teaching." In this instance, that was not the case. Andrew's students' self-assessment of their learning was sophisticated: Yes, they had learned a great deal about the wolves of Ellesmere Island, but they had also learned about the practices of wildlife biologists. Their critique of their learning was that they had not done what they now knew practitioners actually do to make knowledge in the discipline they were studying. In this critique, Andrew saw evidence of students' learning that machine-scored tests cannot detect, are not designed to detect. It is the kind of learning that cognitive psychology has dubbed *metacognition*, "knowing about knowing." Andrew's fifth graders understood the difference between producing knowledge through disciplinary practices and learning the knowledge that others working in the discipline had already produced. They wanted to be *practitioners* of the discipline, not just observers of other practitioners' work. When Andrew developed instruction that addressed their concern, he was in effect teaching them how to continue to use the practices of biologists on their own, in their lives outside of school. As we indicated in the introduction to this book, in the modern world, where information increases minute by minute, it isn't sufficient for us to ask students to learn a body of information and call that an education. Students need to learn how information and knowledge are developed and how information and knowledge will and can continue to be developed. These fifth graders, who learned subject matter by learning and implementing disciplinary practices, including the literacy practices that produced that subject matter, understood that. And they hadn't even read the body of scholarship that argues this case (Bransford, Brown, and Cocking)!

While formative assessment is inseparable from students' and teachers' learning in inquiry-based interdisciplinary projects, in the examples we've just described our purpose has been to draw attention to the fact that activities that figure as formative assessment in these projects often serve multiple functions. As we've just illustrated, in some cases these activities serve simultaneously as formative assessments pinpointing additional work needed for one strand of instruction and as summative assessments for learning in another strand of instruction. For example, the essay Andrew's students wrote about wolves on Ellesmere Island told him what information his students already knew about those wolves and what information he needed to review with them. It also guided his plans for teaching new subject matter: the shaping of essays that dealt with several categories of information about a subject. In some cases, these activities serve simultaneously as unexpected evidence of learning (e.g., Andrew's students' demonstration of their metacognitive learning when he asked them if they felt like wildlife biologists) and as calls for unanticipated enrichment instruction (e.g., the Backyard Biology Project).

In Chapter 4, Trace draws our attention to still other functions that formative assessment plays in shaping instruction in a workshop classroom (see Figure 11). During the Revolution Project, Trace conducted her humanities course as a workshop, in which she conferenced with students in their working groups and individually throughout the project to monitor and support their progress in planning and developing their responses to her assignments. Her instruction took shape in the forms of consulting with and coaching students. While conferencing, consulting, and coaching are for the most part seamless activities, we tease them apart here to draw attention to the functions of each. In *conferences*, Trace was always determining the kind of instruction students needed at that moment in time. She *consulted* with students when they needed encouragement to pursue an effective line of inquiry or composing they had identified and when they needed advice about how to proceed in accomplishing well-aimed plans. And she *coached* students when they needed direct instruction or modeling to complete assignments.

Specifically, Trace read drafts of students' developing writings, made suggestions, and critiqued students' understandings in order to help them prepare for events they planned to stage, documents they designed to "spin," and reports on unfolding events. In one-on-one and in small-group conferences, Trace continually discussed and assessed students' work to fulfill the assignments she had designed for them. In response to these discussions and assessments, Trace offered students direct instruction to support their work. She also used this form of ongoing assessment to return students individually, in groups, and sometimes as a whole class to

Figure 11. Formative assessment and instruction in Trace's workshop classroom.

- Conferencing with students to strengthen their reading and writing
- Consulting with students to encourage and advise for next steps
- Coaching students to see themselves as historians and writers

documents and specific passages they had read earlier in the year that their current work had prepared them to read with increased understanding or that spoke directly to the project they were trying to accomplish. Trace tells us that she used the formative assessments she developed during conferences not just to strengthen emerging drafts of students' work-in-progress and to engage them in purposeful review of historical documents and literary works they had studied across the school year, but also, as a coach might, to encourage them to see themselves as players in the enterprise of making and documenting history:

> As I developed the unit, I remembered historian Wilfred McClay's description of the "mystic chords of memory" that connect us to the past. McClay's idea of invisible threads of memory connecting humanity throughout time and space is evocative and poetic. By circling back to documents, events, and people we had studied, students might begin not just to understand the events themselves, but also to feel connections between themselves and the people they had studied. My hope was that students, in the context of their imaginative role-playing, would envision themselves picking up those invisible threads, see themselves among the historical figures they had studied. I wanted my students to learn history by taking on the roles of those who had created and recorded history. (p. 67)

In ongoing assessment of her students' work-in-progress, Trace also took advantage of coaching opportunities to model for students' future use how historians conduct research in their field. A telling example of this work in which Trace took on the role of a more experienced co-learner for and with her students occurred when the eighth-grade Revolutionaries thought they had gained enough popularity to persuade groups of workers to strike in support of their causes and then found themselves at a standstill because they didn't know how to harness that support. At that moment, the Revolutionaries had little understanding of what strikes entail, how unions function, and how government has traditionally responded to strikes or strike threats. Trace coached her students by modeling how a more experienced learner would approach their situation, demonstrating how experienced learners might assess what they know, what they don't know, and what they need to learn to move forward with their work and learning. As she told us in Chapter 4, Trace hadn't anticipated that the topic of union strikes would emerge in the project, but when it did, she chose to take advantage of the teaching moment. As co-learner—a model learner, in this case—Trace led her students in a process of locating age-appropriate resources that would teach them about the union movement in American history, a topic they had not yet studied. And when it made sense to do so, she offered students direct instruction about unions and union strikes. Trace not only engaged in continual assessment of what students needed to know, but she also taught them how to learn what they needed to know. She introduced them to databases, helped them learn how to search those resources, and led them in shaping and pursuing questions for study in the discipline of history: *What are union strikes? How are they organized? How have they been dealt with? How effective are they?*

Self-Assessment in Inquiry-Based Interdisciplinary Projects

We want to also draw attention to the role that students' self-assessment of their learning often plays as formative assessment in inquiry-based interdisciplinary projects. Because project method teaching positions students in the roles of individuals who have genuine tasks to accomplish rather than, for example, sets of terms and their definitions to memorize or facts to remember and repeat, students often keep their own fingers on the pulse of their progress. This is especially true for projects in which students engage as collaborative learners who discuss their learning with one another on an ongoing basis. Think, for example, of Andrew's fifth-grade students' assessment of their learning that sent him back to the drawing board to develop the Backyard Biology Project.

Trace also invited students to assess their learning in the Revolution Project. At the end of the project, for example, she asked groups to make presentations to the class in which they described what they had accomplished, citing specific artifacts (e.g., speeches, news articles) as proof. In response to a questionnaire she developed, students reflected on what they had learned from participating in the project and what advice they would offer themselves and their classmates were they to repeat the project work. The following excerpts from several students' responses to the questionnaire reveal a bit about what they thought they learned about the literacy practices their class employed in the Revolution Project:

> If I were to switch roles with my counterpart, the advice I would give him would be that he or she should have created more articles about what the government is doing wrong. They could have been more specific.

Make sure that the stories (and propaganda) you write to show the problems in our society are believable to the people. If the story is so unbelievable then people would start to become suspicious and think they were being lied to, which could lead to a loss of power in the government, or if you're a revolutionary, nobody will take you seriously.

If you are a revolutionary, don't have violent protests, don't act powerful, because the government and the media want to feel like they have all the power. You should always have good examples and proof to back you up. But if you're full of yourself, nobody will want to follow you.

Be very organized and rehearse before events like debates and press conferences. Make sure your information is true. Prepare to have a comeback for everything! And because we didn't, it made us look bad and unprepared sometimes, which is not good, especially for government officials.

When Andrew asked his students to tell him how their experience playing wildlife biologists worked for them in the Wolf Project, and when Trace asked student groups to assess their group accomplishments and as individuals to write about their work in the Revolution Project, they engaged students in just a few examples of a host of writing-to-learn strategies developed and circulated in the WAC movement to help us engage our students in self-assessment of their learning. Take, for example, strategies like these in which WAC proponents invited their students to write to learn: write a one-minute essay explaining what you learned during this class period; leave an index card noting things that confused you in a box at the door before leaving class; turn to a partner with a confusion you have about our work today, and if your partner can't answer your question, pose it to the whole class. Strategies like these that encourage students to assess their learning and, in cases where it makes sense, to preserve their anonymity as they do so, invite students, whether in talk or writing (e.g., a colloquy in a small group, a questionnaire, a written reflection), to become self-aware, metacognitive learners even as they purposefully guide our instruction by informing us of the understandings our students are or are not developing.

The work that Trace and Andrew asked of their students in the Revolution Project and the Wolf Project also implicitly asked students to assess their own work as they prepared to make it public. Because inquiry-based interdisciplinary projects are, after all, product and/or action oriented—because there is something to make, some goal to accomplish—teachers typically construct these projects to extend the audience for students' work beyond themselves. The benefits of extending the audience for students' work beyond their classroom teachers is yet another lesson we teachers of literacy learned from the WAC movement.

In project method instruction, students generally develop their work together, and it is witnessed by fellow students and, more often than not, by their school community and parents and guardians who attend events that students stage, or witness displays they construct, or read writings—posters, graphs, charts, letters, poems—they compose to demonstrate their learning. Throughout Trace's project, students assessed their own and one another's work as they fulfilled their assignments, because each group's successful fulfillment of its assignment depended on the other groups' fulfillment of their assignments. If one group's speech was vague or if its information was inaccurate, an opposing group would likely challenge its ideas or facts. If another group's speech or news article was unpersuasive or ineffective, it would not generate the response its authors were seeking. It would flop. So in the process of debating and attempting finally to negotiate with each other, students had to assess their own and one another's content knowledge and literacy skills as they composed their texts. In similar fashion, when Andrew's students took on their roles as workers in the disciplines of wildlife biology and politics, they had to assess their knowledge and powers of persuasion as they worked in congressional committees to enlist their peers' support for their positions and viewpoints and in preparation for presenting their arguments in the mock session of the House of Representatives that they staged for parents and friends.

We've taken the time to describe in some detail activities and judgments that are aptly called teachers' formative assessments of and instructional responses to students' learning because, while they are not unique to the inquiry-based interdisciplinary project method teaching we've described here, they are inseparable from it. And while formative assessment conducted in the context of classroom instruction is one important way teachers learn for and with students, it is certainly not the only way we learn to benefit our students' learning. NCTE's *Literacies of Disciplines* policy brief names others, among them: in the process of reflecting on our teaching in "school communities, conversations with colleagues, hallway interactions with students, or through professional development opportunities like workshops, inservices, or classes" (2).

We also want to take time to describe just one kind of professional development context in which we participate to learn for our students, because it has been particularly productive for us. We speak of the professional learning community known as the National Writing Project (NWP). Many of us today are asked or required to participate in professional learning communities in our home schools or schools districts. We hope that teachers in these PLCs will be able to share and discuss teaching strategies that engage students in learning the literacies of disciplines and the subject matter they produce. Because the NWP has developed a generative model for this work that hundreds of thousands of teachers have benefited from, we don't have to reinvent the wheel.

Professional Learning Communities: Learning with Our Colleagues

In Chapter 2, Patti describes how teachers circulate effective teaching practices for peer review and community use in the NWP. In teaching workshops and critical discussions of them in professional learning communities like the NWP, teachers engage one another in demonstration and discussion of strategies that have proved productive in our individual teaching practices. Through discussions of these strategies, teachers develop theories that allow us to account for why these practices have proved successful and to develop plans for adapting them for use in other units of study, at other levels of instruction, in both general education and subject area courses (Stock, "North American").

For example, recently at the University of Maryland NWP site (UMdWP), when teachers experienced how role-play engaged Andrew's students in the literacy practices of disciplines (biology and history) to create a foundation of knowledge on which they could stand and pivot to learn subject matter for which they did not already possess necessary prior knowledge, they discussed the functions that role-play might serve as a teaching strategy in their own classrooms. They made discoveries like those Andrew named earlier: In the Wolf Project, role-play served a number of functions. It provided students inviting and genuinely engaging purposes for practicing the literacies of discipline-based scholars and professionals whose work paved the way for theirs. It motivated students to become participants in discourses about real issues and to use reading, writing, speaking, and listening to develop understandings of situations and to craft reasonable responses to them. When students discovered that adult specialists in the world beyond school had worked on the issues they were working on, it sparked their interest in learning the subject matter of those literacies. Students genuinely wanted to learn how specialists in the field addressed the problems they themselves were tackling.

Unlike participants in the workshop Patti describes in Chapter 2, all of whom had prior experience of the subject to draw on when they began their study of children's play, Andrew's students did not bring prior knowledge of wolves to the Wolf Project. Because formal instruction is often necessary to provide students background knowledge that makes it possible for them to learn subject matter in school (Moje, "Developing"), Andrew designed classroom instruction to ensure that his students would be able themselves to develop the knowledge about wolves they would need to proceed successfully in their studies. He asked students to take on the role of wildlife biologists, to dress the part, embark on a virtual field trip, pitch tents, and, with field notebooks in hand, use the literacy practices of wildlife biologists to construct a body of foundational knowledge about wolves. In the spirit of play—play that Jerome Bruner would call serious business—these fifth graders used literacy practices developed in the discipline of biology to construct knowledge necessary for their continued learning about wolves. Then, standing on the ground of this foundational knowledge, the students "pivoted," left the wild, entered libraries, and used literacy practices developed by historians to construct knowledge about the existence and disappearance of wolves in the lower 48 states. Rooted now in this enriched and extended grounding of knowledge, students pivoted again, and, taking on the role of legislators, they used the literacy practices of the US House of Representatives to develop and pass a Wolf Conservation Act that called for the reintroduction of the wolf into the Lower 48. Pivoting one last time, they became biologists who worked to locate wolves for reintroduction.

Likewise, when Trace recently introduced colleagues in the Hudson Valley Writing Project (HVWP) to how she used role-play to engage students in the Revolution Project, participants were able to experience and discuss yet another function that role-play serves in learning the literacy practices of disciplines. Rather than asking her students to pivot from taking on the role and using the literacy practices of workers in one discipline (e.g., biology) to taking on the role and using the literacy practices in another discipline (e.g., history) to accomplish a complex project, Trace asked her eighth graders to "blend" literacy practices from several disciplines (i.e., history and literary, composition, and rhetorical studies) to develop interpretations of the roles they would play in the project and to work to fulfill those roles. Participants in her workshop discussed the reasons why Trace asked students to regard the boundaries between literacy practices of disciplines as flexible and porous (*Literacies* of *Disciplines*, 1). She explained that, first, she wanted students to feel passionately connected to the past—to historical figures, events, and circumstances—just as they do to characters, plots, and settings in the imaginative literature they like to read. Second, she wanted to help students develop close, critical readings of accounts of history, to make them aware that documented history is not a monolithic record of one true version of events, figures, and circumstances, but instead a body of inscribed interpretations of available data and accounts of what happened in the past. And third, she wanted them to apply the critical reading strategies and figurative uses of language they had learned in literary, composition, and rhetorical studies to their writing of history. In effect, by asking students to bring the literacy practices of literary, composition, and rhetorical studies to bear on their study of history, Trace prompted them to observe the differences among different disciplines' literacy practices and to be aware of when they and others use those practices, why, and to what effect.

Colleagues who have participated in the workshops we have offered in professional learning community sites like the NWP have experienced what we have described in this book: the primary reasons we engage our students in inquiry-based interdisciplinary projects. For us those reasons are these: Projects like the ones we have described inspire students to be active, even enthusiastic, participants in their learning. They position students to be makers of the subject matter knowledge they are required to learn. And they enable students to see the value of subject matter content *and* the literacy practices that different disciplines lend to their project work, as well as the differences between them.

It is important to note here that in professional learning communities where we are able to share and discuss our teaching practices with one another, teachers don't just experience teaching practices, theorize them, and account for why they are sound and effective. We take them home and put them to work to benefit our students' learning. For example, after UMdWP participants learned about the strategies that Andrew uses to engage his students in the literacy practices of wildlife biologists, a teacher of English language learners commented on how useful they would be for her students. Minah observed that viewing the film *White Wolf*, at first without sound, would position her students on an equal playing field with native English speakers, and that the field notebook activities Andrew designed would enable her students to develop English vocabulary and knowledge about wolves. Shana, a third-grade teacher, described how she would adapt Andrew's teaching strategies for use in a Westward Expansion unit of study in her curriculum. Thor, a high school teacher, described how he planned to adapt the strategies to engage his students in an investigation of the bees that are declining in population in the Northeast.

Furthermore, each of those adaptations and others that participants described in turn led the three of us to think of still other promising uses of Andrew's teaching strategies in our own classrooms. In light of Minah's observations, Patti intends to share the *White Wolf* film and field notebook activities with her teacher education students, who have increasing numbers of English language learners in their classes. She also wants to try an "observation slap" and sorting activity in her "Children's Play" workshop after participants share and chart common themes they discover in small-group discussions of their play experiences. She thinks such an "observation slap" and sorting activity will allow workshop participants to develop the super- and subordinate themes that she is currently taking the lead in developing in her workshop.

Additionally, we continue to learn from own practices as we prepare to share them with colleagues. For example, as he prepared to share his Wolf Project, Andrew identified, theorized, and named the process that enables his students to better understand the differences between the disciplines of literacies and the subject matter knowledge they produce: *pivoting*. He developed this unit of study to enable his students to practice the literacies of different disciplines and, as they practiced the literacy of first one and then another discipline, to construct along the way the knowledge necessary for them to proceed in their study. But until he prepared to share his practice with colleagues, he had not accounted for or named the process that secured students' understanding of differences between the literacies of disciplines and the different bodies of knowledge they produce. In the theorizing and naming, he and we learned a bit more about how to teach the literacies of disciplines.

By describing how we use formative assessment and how we have participated in one professional learning community, the National Writing Project, we have tried to illustrate just two of the ways in which we and numerous other teachers continue to be learners for and with our students for the benefit of their learning. In the spirit of our commitment to continue to reflect on our practice and to examine it with colleagues, we conclude our book by returning to the place we began.

Ongoing Questions

We conclude with the questions we posed to introduce our book because we continue to be confronted by them and to work to address them:

> What do curricula and instruction look like that are theoretically sound, that are recommended by research in education, *and* that fulfill current legislated requirements for students' literacy and subject matter learning experiences? And, in particular, what do they look like when those requirements named in the Common Core State Standards for English Language Arts & Literacy in History/Social Studies, Science (NGO and CCSSO), and Technical Subjects emphasize the importance of having students read and write information-rich texts in multiple genres and media?

The inquiry-based interdisciplinary projects we have shared here are one way that we are working to answer these questions. We have described them hoping that you—colleagues also committed to learning for and with students—will share your efforts to answer these questions in NCTE convention sessions, NWP institutes, PLCs in your home communities, and countless other venues for the benefit of our students' learning. In each of the examples we described, we engaged students in the literacy practices of disciplines as a means of solving real problems and learning the subject matter that those practices construct.

And we continue to wonder if a shift of focus in instruction—from asking students to remember and repeat information to asking them to use the practices of discipline-based workers to discover and construct information—might prompt change of thought patterns in the field of education like those Heisenberg described in science. And we wonder what it will take to make such a shift in instruction a reality for more teachers.

We wonder.

Annotated Bibliography

Discipline-Based Literacy Instruction

Subject Matter Approach to Discipline-Based Literacy Instruction

Grant, Maria C., and Douglas Fisher
Reading and Writing in Science: Tools to Develop Disciplinary Literacy.
Thousand Oaks: Corwin, 2010. Print.

A professor of literacy education and a professor of science education take us into the classrooms of science teachers who are engaging their students in research-based science teaching that focuses on science literacy. In addition to covering the requisite subject matter, the book describes teachers intent on enabling students to continue to learn, reflect, and communicate about science throughout their lives.

Moje, Elizabeth Birr
"Foregrounding the Disciplines in Secondary Literacy Teaching and Learning: A Call for Change."
Journal of Adolescent and Adult Literacy 52:2 (2008): 96–107. Print.

In this and her many other excellent essays, Moje reports and argues for the body of research that supports the teaching we describe in our book. She calls for teaching subject matter by teaching the disciplinary-based practices—including the literacy practices—that produced it. For anyone interested in teaching the literacies of disciplines Moje is a must-read.

Ogle, Donna, Ron Klemp, and Bill McBride
Building Literacy in Social Studies: Strategies for Improving Comprehension and Critical Thinking.
Alexandria, VA: ASCD, 2007. Print.

This book focuses specifically on building vocabulary and literacy skills and working with primary and secondary source documents, newspapers, and Internet sources in teaching social studies. The authors include examples of classroom teaching that highlight the building of these skills in cooperative and collaborative learning contexts.

Rothstein, Andrew, Evelyn Rothstein, and Gerald Lauber
Write for Mathematics. **2nd ed.**
Thousand Oaks, Corwin, 2007. Print.

In addressing NCTM standards, this book presents ten writing strategies designed to help students learn mathematical concepts and theories and offers teachers advice on how to incorporate the math standards into their curricula. The strategies focus on helping students develop conceptual understandings of the subject matter.

Shanahan, Timothy, and Cynthia Shanahan
"Teaching Disciplinary Literacy to Adolescents: Rethinking Content-Area Literacy."
Harvard Educational Review 78:1 (2008): 40–59. Print.

Cited widely in discussions of discipline-based literacy teaching, the authors of this article report a study they conducted demonstrating that practitioners in mathematics, chemistry, and history read texts differently. The study led the authors, experts in the field, and secondary school teachers to recommend that subject area teachers teach their students different reading strategies in different subject areas.

White, James Boyd
"The Invisible Discourse of the Law: Reflections on Legal Literacy and General Education." *fforum: Essays on Theory and Practice in the Teaching of Writing.* Ed. Patricia L. Stock.
Montclair: Boynton/Cook, 1983. 46–59. Print.

This classic article remains the clearest, most persuasive argument for teaching literacy in context. White demonstrates with telling examples how in subject matter and disciplinary communities language takes on nuanced meanings that do not hold beyond those communities. The article argues that for individuals to use language effectively in different disciplinary communities, they must learn how the languages of those communities work.

Genre Approach to Discipline-Based Literacy Instruction

Devitt, Amy J.
Writing Genres.
Carbondale: Southern Illinois UP, 2004. Print.

This book poses and illustrates a rhetorical theory of genre that defines genres as social actions and traces the development of genre research. To illustrate the theory she poses—one that resonates with the workshop Bernard Van't Hul developed in the 1970s that Patti describes in Chapter 1—Devitt reports on her study of the genres developed and used in a community of tax accountants.

Fleischer, Cathy, and Sarah Andrew-Vaughn
Writing Outside Your Comfort Zone: Helping Students Navigate Unfamiliar Genres.
Portsmouth: Heinemann, 2009. Print.

Fleischer and Andrew-Vaughn report on work in which they have asked each student in their college-level and high school classrooms to choose and study a genre unfamiliar to them, to read lots of examples of it, to identify its distinguishing features, to think about why those features characterize the genre, and to try their hands at writing the genre themselves. The book provides fully detailed outlines and examples of how other teachers might conduct an "unfamiliar genre project" in their classrooms.

Lattimer, Heather
Thinking through Genre: Units of Study in Reading and Writing Workshops 4–12.
Portland: Stenhouse, 2003. Print.

Thinking through Genre is a valuable resource for teachers of English language arts who want to introduce their students to the literacies of disciplines by having students read and write in a variety of genres. The book offers rich examples of six fully developed units of study appropriate for use in English language arts classrooms.

Interdisciplinary Resources

Beane, James A.
Curriculum Integration: Designing the Core of Democratic Education.
New York: Teachers College Press, 1997. Print.

Beane traces the history of interdisciplinary instruction and the theory supporting it. He also provides helpful classroom examples of interdisciplinary teaching and shows how the disciplines can connect thematically in interdisciplinary units of study.

Drake, Susan, and Rebecca Burns
Meeting Standards through Integrated Curriculum.
Alexandria: ASCD, 2004. Print.

Drake and Burns provide a strong rationale for integrated curricula and interdisciplinary learning. They also offer helpful advice about how to link interdisciplinary work to a standards-based curriculum, and they present models of the teaching they recommend.

Erickson, H. Lynn
Concept-Based Curriculum and Instruction: Teaching beyond the Facts.
Thousand Oaks: Corwin, 2002. Print.

This book offers a strong rationale for organizing curricula around important concepts that can be approached across the disciplines. As he aligns curriculum design with standards, Erickson shows how teachers can help students develop disciplinary knowledge and conceptual understanding while offering high-quality instruction across the content areas.

Five, Cora Lee, and Marie Dionisio
Bridging the Gap: Integrating Curriculum in Upper Elementary and Middle Schools.
Portsmouth: Heinemann, 1996. Print.

Five and Dionisio describe helping their students make thematic connections across disciplines, pursue their own inquiries, and participate actively in an American Revolution curriculum. The authors detail their experiments and discoveries and also provide helpful suggestions for others striving to bring curriculum to life.

Lapp, Diane, James Flood, and Nancy Farnan
Content Area Reading and Learning. 3rd. ed.
New York: Routledge, 2008. Print.

This book is a collection of articles that offer a wealth of classroom strategies for helping middle and secondary school students develop content concepts and practices for lifelong learning in the disciplines. The book also includes excellent discussions of the theory supporting the strategies described. The articles are both general and content area specific.

Writing Across the Curriculum

Britton, James, Tony Burgess, Nancy Martin, Alex McLeod, and Harold Rosen
The Development of Writing Abilities (11–18).
London: Macmillan, 1975. Print.

This book reports on the study conducted by Britton and his colleagues from 1966 to 1971 in a Schools Council Project based at the University of London Institute of Education. The project is often described as launching the Writing Across the Curriculum movement. Britton and his colleagues argue that language—in all its forms—is our most readily available, most powerful means of learning and is too seldom used for that purpose in classrooms.

Stock, Patricia .L.
fforum: Essays on Theory and Practice in the Teaching of Writing.
Montclair: Boynton/Cook, 1983. Print.

Published when the influence of the Writing Across the Curriculum movement was taking strong hold in the United States, this book is a collection of essays written by the movement's major voices, including Britton, Martin, Graves, Murray, Elbow, Fulwiler, Macrorie, Coles, Bartholomae, Moffett, and Fader. It also includes James Boyd White's classic article that demonstrates as well, if not better, than anything written since why literacy learning in context matters.

Zawacki, Terry Myers, and Paul M. Rogers, eds.
Writing Across the Curriculum: A Critical Sourcebook.
Boston: Bedford/St. Martin's, 2012. Print.

This collection of essays provides the most recent history of the Writing Across the Curriculum movement and its evolution. It also includes classic articles published earlier in *College English*, *College Composition and Communication*, etc. The articles describe WAC strategies developed for use in both postsecondary and secondary school classrooms.

Formative Assessment

Andrade, Heidi L., and Gregory J. Cizek, eds.
Handbook of Formative Assessment.
New York: Routledge, 2010. Print.

In nineteen articles, this collection documents the growth of the formative assessment movement across the globe. As educators and policymakers come to grips with the limited value of summative assessments for improving instruction and learning, this rich resource highlights what those in the formative assessment movement are learning that might benefit student learning.

Filkins, Scott
Beyond Standardized Truth: Improving Teaching and Learning through Inquiry-Based Reading Assessment.
Urbana: NCTE, 2012. Print.

Filkins's award-winning book takes us into his and colleagues' classrooms to see how secondary school teachers across the curriculum engage in inquiry-based assessment of learning for their students' benefit. This book is as theoretically informed as it is classroom teacher–oriented.

McMillan, James H., ed.
Formative Classroom Assessment: Theory into Practice.
New York: Teachers College Press, 2007. Print.

In this collection of essays, well-known experts demonstrate how to implement formative assessment strategies in science, English, social studies, and mathematics classrooms to benefit students' efforts and achievement.

Professional Learning Communities

Gray, James
Teachers at the Center: A Memoir of the Early Years of the National Writing Project.
Berkeley: NWP, 2000. Print.

James Gray's memoir documents the establishment, growth, and development of a professional learning community in education, the National Writing Project. The project began as a local San Francisco Bay Area gathering of teachers who taught one another and studied their own best practices for teaching writing and developed defining practices for their scholarship. Gray shows how this early work then expanded, first into a regional, then a national, and ultimately an international professional learning community.

Wenger, Étienne
Communities of Practice: Learning, Meaning, and Identity.
New York: Cambridge UP, 1998. Print.

We describe only one, but any of the books by Étienne Wenger and/or his frequent coauthor Jean Lave, offer examples of the theory they developed: in communities of practice, groups of people who share common concerns or practices learn from one another how to do their work more effectively as they interact and, in the process, teach and learn from one another.

Works Cited

Bakhtin, M. M. *Speech Genres and Other Late Essays*. Trans. Vern W. McGee. Ed. Caryl Emerson and Michael Holquist. Austin: U of Texas P, 1986. Print.

Berthoff, Ann E. *Forming, Thinking, Writing: The Composing Imagination*. Montclair: Boynton/Cook, 1982. Print.

Boshara, Ray. "Poverty Is More Than a Matter of Income." *New York Times*. New York Times, 29 Sept. 2002. Web. 14 Jan. 2014.

Bransford, John D., Ann L. Brown, and Rodney R. Cocking. *How People Learn: Brain, Mind, Experience, and School*. Washington, DC: US Natl. Acad., 1999. Print.

Britton, James. *Language and Learning*. Coral Gables: U of Miami P, 1970. Print.

Britton, James, Tony Burgess, Nancy Martin, Alex McLeod, and Harold Rosen. *The Development of Writing Abilities (11–18)*. London: Macmillan, 1975. Print.

Bruner, Jerome. "Play Is Serious Business." *Psychology Today* Jan. 1975: 80–83. Print.

Cler, S., and K. Ronsheimer. "Let's Play: A Unit Designed Primarily for 9th Grade, and Adaptable to Other Grade Levels." San Jose: San Jose Area Writing Project, 2004. Print.

Darwin, Charles. *Journal of Researches into the Natural History and Geology of the Countries Visited during the Voyage of H.M.S. Beagle Round the World, under the Command of Capt. FitzRoy, R.N*. London: Murray, 1845. Print.

———. *On the Origin of Species by Means of Natural Selection, or the Preservation of Favoured Races in the Struggle for Life*. London: Murray, 1859. Print.

Devitt, Amy J. *Writing Genres*. Carbondale: Southern Illinois UP, 2004. Print.

Dewey, John. *Democracy and Education*. New York: Macmillan, 1916. Print.

Eakin, Emily. "On the Dark Side of Democracy." *New York Times*. New York Times, 31 Jan. 2004. Web. 14 Jan. 2012.

Elbow, Peter. *Writing without Teachers*. New York: Oxford UP, 1973. Print.

Fulwiler, Toby, ed. *The Journal Book*. Portsmouth: Heinemann, 1987. Print.

Gee, James Paul. *What Video Games Have to Teach Us about Learning and Literacy*. New York: Palgrave-Macmillan. 2007. Print.

Gere, Anne Ruggles. *Roots in the Sawdust: Writing to Learn Across the Disciplines*. Urbana: NCTE, 1985. Print.

Goodenough, Elizabeth, ed. *Secret Spaces of Childhood*. Ann Arbor: U of Michigan P, 2003. Print.

Goodman, Ken. *On Reading*. Portsmouth: Heinemann, 1996. Print.

Gordon, Jane. "At Hospitals, A Cushion for the Poor." *New York Times*. New York Times, 8 June 2003. Web. 14 Jan. 2014.

Hakim, Joy. "Reading, Writing, and…History." *History Matters* Apr. 1996. Web.

Heath, Shirley Brice. "The Education of a Teacher: Shaping a Creative Tension between General and Professional Education." *Tension and Dynamism: The Education of a Teacher* [conference proceedings]. Ed. Patricia Lambert Stock. Ann Arbor: U of Michigan, School of Education, 1986. Print.

Isidore, Chris. "Economists Mixed on Kerry Plan: Conservatives Applaud Cut in Corporate Taxes, but Even Liberals Doubt It Would Stop Outsourcing." *CNN/Money*. Cable News Network, 26 March 2004. Web. 19 Dec. 2013.

Kennedy, Robert F. Jr., and Dennis Rivera. "Pollution's Chief Victims: The Poor." *New York Times*. New York Times, 15 Aug. 1992. Web. 14 Jan. 2014.

Kilpatrick, William H. "The Project Method." *Teachers College Record* 19.4 (1918): 319–34. Print.

Kirby, Dan, and Tom Liner. *Inside Out: Developmental Strategies for Teaching Writing*. Montclair: Boynton/Cook, 1981. Print.

Knoll, Michael. "'I had made a mistake': William H. Kilpatrick and the Project Method." *Teachers College Record*. 114.2 (2012): 1–45. Print.

Kozol, Jonathan. *Amazing Grace: The Lives of Children*

and the Conscience of a Nation. New York: Harper-Perennial, 1995. Print.

———. *Savage Inequalities: Children in America's Schools*. New York: HarperPerennial, 1991. Print.

Kuhn, Thomas S. *The Structure of Scientific Revolutions*. 2nd ed. Chicago: U of Chicago P, 1970. Print.

Lave, Jean, and Etienne Wenger. *Situated Learning: Legitimate Peripheral Participation*. New York: Cambridge UP, 1991. Print.

Macrorie, Ken. *Telling Writing*. 4th ed. Upper Montclair: Boynton/Cook, 1985. Print.

Mayberry, Robert M., David A. Nicewander, Huanying Qin, and David J. Ballard. "Improving Quality and Reducing Inequities: A Challenge in Achieving Best Care." *Baylor University Medical Center Proceedings* 19.2 (2006): 103–18. Print.

McClay, Wilfred, M. "Acquiring Historical Consciousness: The Mystic Chords of Memory." *History Matters* Oct. 1996. Web. 2004–2005.

McNamee, Thomas. *The Return of the Wolf to Yellowstone*. New York: Holt, 1997. Print.

Meyer, Jan H. F., and Ray Land, eds. *Overcoming Barriers to Student Understanding: Threshold Concepts and Troublesome Knowledge*. New York: Routledge, 2006. Print.

Miller, Carolyn R. "Genre as Social Action." *Quarterly Journal of Speech* 70 (1984): 151–67. Print.

Moffett, James. *Active Voice: A Writing Program Across the Curriculum*. Montclair: Boynton/Cook, 1981. Print.

Moje, Elizabeth Birr. "Developing Disciplinary Discourses, Literacies, and Identities: What's Knowledge Got to Do with It?" *Discourses and Identities in Contexts of Educational Change: Contributions from the United States and Mexico*. Ed. Guadalup López-Bonilla and Karen Englander. New York: Lang, 2011. 49–74. Print.

———. "Foregrounding the Disciplines in Secondary Literacy Teaching and Learning: A Call for Change." *Journal of Adolescent and Adult Literacy* 52.2 (2008): 96–107. Print.

Nagourney, Adam, and Diane Cardwell. "Democrats in Debate Clash over Iraq War." *New York Times*. New York Times, 27 Oct. 2003. Web. 14 Jan. 2014.

National Council of Teachers of English. *Literacies of Disciplines: An NCTE Policy Research Brief*. Urbana: NCTE, Sept. 2011. Web.

National Governors Association (NGO) and Council of Chief State School Officers (CCSSO). *Common Core State Standards for English Language Arts & Literacy in History/Social Studies, Science, and Technical Subjects*. June 2010. Web.

Obama, Barack. "Remarks to the Democratic National Convention." *New York Times*. New York Times, 27 July 2004. Web. 14 Jan. 2014.

Schmidt, William H. "Inequality in the American Education System." *Huffington Post* 17 July 2012. Web. 1 Jan. 2014.

Shanahan, Timothy, and Cynthia Shanahan. "Teaching Disciplinary Literacy to Adolescents: Rethinking Content-Area Literacy." *Harvard Educational Review* 78:1 (2008): 40–59. Print.

Shiels, Merrill. "Why Johnny Can't Write." *Newsweek* 8 Dec. 1975: 58–65. Print.

Simon, Herbert A. *The Sciences of the Artificial*. 3rd ed. Cambridge: MIT P, 1996. Print.

Stock, Patricia L., ed. *fforum: Essays on Theory and Practice in the Teaching of Writing*. Montclair: Boynton/Cook, 1983. Print.

———. "The North American Teacher Research Movement: The National Writing Project and the Scholarship of Teaching Practice." *International Perspectives on Teaching English in a Globalised World*. Ed. Andrew Goodwyn, Louann Reid, and Cal Durrant. New York: Routledge, 2014. 188–98. Print

———. "Toward a Theory of Genre in Teacher Research: Contributions from a Reflective Practitioner." *English Education* 33.2 (2001): 100–14. Print.

Street, Brian V. *Literacy in Theory and Practice*. New York: Cambridge UP, 1984. Print.

Student Press Initiative. *About Face: Portraits of Activism*. New York: Student Press Initiative, 2007. Print.

———. *Magpie: Who's Changing My Hood?* New York: Student Press Initiative, 2007. Print.

Thorne, Barrie. *Gender Play: Girls and Boys in School*. New Brunswick: Rutgers UP, 1993. Print.

Tough, Paul. "The Harlem Project." *New York Times*. New York Times, 20 June 2004. Web. 14

Jan. 2014.

Tuhus, Melinda. "Battling Dumpsites in Poor Neighborhoods." *New York Times*. New York Times, 30 June 1996. Web. 14 Jan. 2014.

United States Dept. of the Interior. Fish and Wildlife Service. "Gray Wolf Range in the Contiguous United States." *FWS*.gov. US Fish and Wildlife Service, Jan. 2009. Web. 4 June 2013.

———. *The Reintroduction of Gray Wolves to Yellowstone National Park and Central Idaho: Final Environmental Impact Statement*. Helena: Region 6, U.S. Fish and Wildlife Service, 1994. Print.

———. National Park Service. *Yellowstone Resources and Issues Handbook 2012: An Annual Compendium of Information about Yellowstone National Park*. 2012. Web. 10 Jan. 2014.

Vygotsky, L. S. (1978). *Mind in Society: The Development of Higher Psychological Processes*. Cambridge: Harvard UP, 1978. Print.

———. *Thought and Language*. Cambridge: MIT P, 1986. Print.

Wenger, Étienne. *Communities of Practice: Learning, Meaning, and Identity*. New York: Cambridge UP, 1998. Print.

White, James Boyd. "The Invisible Discourse of the Law: Reflections on Legal Literacy and General Education." Stock, *fforum* 46–59.

White Wolf. Prod. Robin Hellier and Jim Brandenburg. National Geographic Society, 1988. Video.

Wilhelm, Jeffrey D. *Engaging Readers and Writers with Inquiry: Promoting Deep Understandings in Language Arts and the Content Areas with Guiding Questions*. New York: Scholastic, 2007. Print.

———. *"You Gotta BE the Book": Teaching Engaged and Reflective Reading with Adolescents*. New York: Teachers College Press; Urbana: NCTE, 1997. Print.

Winter, Greg. "Long after Brown v. Board of Education, Sides Switch." *New York Times*. New York Times, 16 May 2004. Web. 14 Jan. 2014.

Yardley, Jim. "A City Struggles to Provide Health Care Pledged by U.S." *New York Times*. New York Times, 7 Aug. 2001. Web. 14 Jan. 2014.

Zawacki, Terry Myers, and Paul M. Rogers, eds. *Writing Across the Curriculum: A Critical Sourcebook*. Boston: Bedford/St. Martin's, 2012. Print.

Zinn, Howard, and Anthony Arnove. *Voices of a People's History of the United States*. New York: Seven Stories, 2004. Print.

Index

Activity theory, 7
Andrade, H. L., 99
Andrew-Vaughn, S., 98
Aristotle, 7
Arnove, A., 69
Author's perspective, in historical accounts, 66

Backyard Biology Project, 43–45, 86–87, 90
Ballard D. J., 77
Beane, J. A., 98
Becker, J. E., 50
Berthoff, A. E., 4
Blau, S., 11
Boshara, R., 78
Brandenburg, J., 38
Bransford, J. D., xxii, 87
Bristow, C., 2
Britton, J., 2, 3, 4, 43, 99
Brown, A. L., xxii, 87
Bruner, J., 31, 32, 92
Burgess, T., 3, 99
Burns, R., 98

Cardwell, D., 79
Carter, M., xi
Chesnut, M., 63
Cizek, G. J., 99
Cler, S., 26, 27
Cocking, R. R., xxii, 87
Common Core State Standards (CCSS), xiii, xvii, 24, 27, 36, 47, 60, 83
    implications for curriculum, xvii
Communities of practice, 7–8
Correspondence, writing, 20–22
Criticism, writing, 22–23
cummings, e. e., 69
Curriculum, xvii, 36
    Common Core State Standards implications for, xvii
    fifth-grade, 36

Devitt, A. J., 98

Dewey, J., xx, 59, 60, 83
Diaries, of historical figures, 63
Dionisio, M., 99
Disciplines, xi, xii–xiii, xix–xxiii
    boundaries of, xix–xxiii
    complications of term, xi, 8
    development of knowledge about, 12
    versus fields, xx
    literacies of, xii–xiii, 7–8
    theorizing in, 21
Douglass, F., 64
Drake, S., 98
Dylan, B., 69

Eakin, E., 78
Ecosystems, student research into, 45–48
Education, inequity in, 77
Elbow, P., 4
Endangered Species Act, 36
Erikson, H. L., 98

Farnan, N., 99
Ferguson, C., 33
Filkins, S., 100
Fisher, D., 97
Five, C. L., 99
Fleischer, C., 98
Flood, J., 99
Formative assessment, 84–91
    in Backyard Biology Project, 86–87, 89
    in Revolution Project, 87–89, 90
    in Wolf Project, 84–86, 90
Frank, A., 63
Freud, S., 18
Fulwiler, T., 4

Gee, J. P., 9, 38
Genre studies, 7
Gere, A. R., 4
Goodall, J., 31
Goodenough, E., 23, 24, 25, 28, 30
Goodman, K., 50

Gordon, J., 78
Grant, M., 97
Gray, J., 99

Hakim, J., 61
Health care, inequity in, 77, 78
Heath, S. B., 82, 83
Historical research, 49–51, 58
History, 58–59, 63–64
    literacy instruction in, 58–59. *See also* Revolution Project
    rhetorical approach to, 63
Hudson Valley Writing Project (HVWP), 93
Humanities, teaching, 60–62

Inquiry-based projects, xxi
Intentional teaching, modeling of, 20
International Reading Association, 60
Isidore, C., 78

Jefferson, T., 64
Jigsaw Project, 26–27

Kalman, B., 50
Kennedy, R. F., Jr., 77
Kilpatrick, W., xx, xxi, 60, 83
Kirby, D., 2
Klemp, R., 97
Knowledge, construction of, 12
Kozol, J., 77, 78
Kuhn, T., 41

Land, R., 2
Language, xvii–xviii, 2
    discipline-specific, xvii–xviii, 12, 41
    historical literacy goals for, 61–62
    as powerful learning tool, 2
    of revolution, 64
Lapp, D., 99
Lattimer, H., 98
Lauber, G., 97
Lave, J., 7
Learning, through play, 32
Lease, M. E., 69
Liner, T., 4

Literacies of *Disciplines* (NCTE), xi–xv, xvii, xviii, 11, 35, 58, 60, 83, 84, 91
Literacy(ies), xi–xiii
    development of, 12
    and disciplines, xi
    of disciplines, xii–xiii, 7–8, 38, 83
    pluralities of, xi, xii, xvii–xviii
    research on, xi
Literacy learning, xvii–xviii, xix
    across disciplines, xvii–xviii
    and subject matter learning, xix

Macrorie, K., 4
MAPS, 7
Martin, N., 3, 99
Mayberry, R. M., 77
McBride, B., 97
McClay, W., 67, 88
McLeod, A., 3
McMillan, J. H., 99
McNamee, T., 54
Mech, D. L., 38, 39, 55
Meyer, J. H. F., 2
Miner, V., 25
Mitchell, J. H., 25
Moffett, J., 4
Moje, E. B., xii, 8, 9, 32, 38, 92, 97
Morgan, R., 2
Mother Jones, 69

Nagourney, A., 79
National Council of Social Studies, 60
National Council of Teachers of English (NCTE), xvii, 4, 11, 35, 58, 60, 83, 84, 91, 95
National Research Council, xxi
National Writing Project (NWP), xiii, 2, 4, 13, 91, 92, 95
New literacy studies (NLS), xix, 8–10
Nicewander, D. A., 77

Obama, B., 78
Observation, 38–40, 41–45
    transforming into writing, 41–45
Ogle, D., 97

Play, xix, 12–34. *See also* Role-play
    experimental psychology view of, 31
    learning through, 32
    problem-solving strategies developed through, 31
    prompts for exploring, 12–14
    questions for discussion about, 19
    rationale for studying, 30–34
    role in learning, xix
    themes about, 14–19
    workshop on, 12–30
Poughkeepsie Day School (PDS), 59–60
Problem-solving strategies, development of, 31, 80
Professional learning communities (PLCs), xxiii, 92–95

Qin, H., 77

Read-alouds, 20–21
Research, 49–54, 58
    on government and legislation, 51–54
    historical, 49–51, 58
Revolution Project, 61–81, 87–90, 91
    assignment for, 66–67
    attention to author's perspective in, 66
    final debate in, 79–80
    formative assessment in, 87–89, 89–90, 91
    goals for language use, 61–62
    group assignments for, 68
    negotiations in, 76–79
    preparation for, 62–65
    problem-solving in, 80
    public events in, 67–68, 71–75
    readings for, 69
    role-play in, 66–67
    tactics of groups in, 75–76
    teacher role in, 71–72, 76
Rivera, D., 77
Rogers, P. M., 8, 99
Role-play, xix, 19, 32–33, 37–41, 52–54, 66–67
    generative power of, 32–33
    students acting as specialists through, 37–38, 40, 52–54, 66–67
    as teaching strategy, 32, 33
    themes about, 19
    transforming identity and vision through, 37–41, 52–54

Ronsheimer, K., 26, 27
Rosen, H., 3, 99
Rothstein, A., 97
Rothstein, E., 97

San Jose Area Writing Project (SJAWP), 26
Schmidt, W. H., 77
Secret Spaces of Childhood (Goodenough), 23–24, 25, 26
Self-assessment, student, 89–91
Shanahan, C., 59, 60, 97
Shanahan, T., 59, 60, 97
Shiels, M., 1
Simon, H., xxi, 80
Slam poetry, rhetorical elements of, 64
Sociocultural studies, 8–10
South Coast Writing Project (SCWriP), 11, 12, 13
Stanton, C. S., 64
Stock, P. L., 4, 92
Street, B., 9
Subject areas, xi, xvii–xviii, 12
    development of, 12
    versus disciplines, xi
    language differences across, xvii–xviii
Subject matter learning, xix, xxii, 12, 83
    literacy learning and, xix
Swinburne, S. R., 50

Talk, importance of, 43
Teacher education, changes in, 82–83
Teachers as learners, 83–95
    in formative assessment, 84–91
    in professional learning communities, 92–95
Teaching, intentional, 20
Thorne, B., 19
Threshold concepts, 2
Tough, P., 78
Toxic waste, 77–78
Tuhus, M., 77

University of Maryland Writing Project (UMdWP), 33, 92, 94

Van't Hul, B., 6, 7, 8, 9, 11, 12, 13
Vision, transformation of, 41
Vocabulary, domain-specific, 41

Vygotsky, L. S., 4, 7

Wenger, É., 7, 100
White, J. B., 1, 97
Wilhelm, J., 57, 61
Winter, G., 78
Wolf Project, 36–57, 84–86, 92–93
    Backyard Biology Project and, 43–45
    choice of issues for, 36–37
    ecosystem research for, 45–48
    field notebooks for, 39
    formative assessment in, 84–86, 90
    government and legislation, research into, 51–54
    historical research for, 49–51
    observations for, 38–40, 41–44
    species descriptions and, 45–47
    virtual road trip in, 38

Writing, 25, 40–41
    Common Core State Standards for, 47
    exploring craft of, 25
    revisions, 40–41
Writing Across the Curriculum (WAC) movement, xix, xxiii, 1–7, 83
    overview of, 2, 3-4
    in postsecondary education, 4–5
    two strands of, 2, 4–7
Writing in the Disciplines (WID), 2, 4–7
Writing to Learn (WTL), 2, 4, 12
    genres of, 12, 14, 20, 22
    workshop employing strategies of, 12–30

Yardley, J., 78

Zawacki, T. M., 8, 99
Zinn, H., 69

Authors

Patricia Lambert Stock is professor emerita at Michigan State University, where she served as founding director of the MSU Writing Center and co-founder of the Red Cedar Writing Project. Earlier, she taught secondary school English in New York and Michigan, as well as served on the faculties of the English Composition Board and the Department of English at the University of Michigan and the Department of English and the Writing Program at Syracuse University. A Past President of NCTE, Stock has written more than fifty books and articles on literacy teaching and learning, practitioner research, and the scholarship of teaching.

Trace Schillinger is a secondary educator and the humanities coordinator at Poughkeepsie Day School in New York's Hudson Valley. She also serves as a returning fellow and teacher consultant for the Hudson Valley Writing Project, and she teaches in the Department of Secondary Education at SUNY New Paltz. Schillinger earned her doctorate at Teachers College, Columbia University, and has published articles about teaching poetry in the secondary classroom, integrating technology in the English classroom, and the use of imaginative writing in the history classroom.

Andrew Stock is a public elementary school teacher in New York's Hudson Valley. He has taught in a variety of settings, including children's museums, historic sites, national parks, and universities. His academic background includes a Master of Arts in teaching from the University of New Hampshire, a bachelor of arts in history from the University of Michigan, a year of study at the Moscow State Institute of History and Archives in Russia, and field research at the University of Michigan Biological Station.

This book was typeset in Janson Text and BotonBQ by Barbara Frazier.

Typefaces used on the cover include American Typewriter, Frutiger Bold, Formata Light, and Formata Bold.

The book was printed on 60-lb. White Recycled Offset paper by Versa Press, Inc.

30% Total Recycled Fiber